Postcolonial Preaching

Postcolonial and Decolonial Studies in Religion and Theology

Series Editor: Sheryl Kujawa-Holbrook, Claremont School of Theology

Series Editorial Board
Jon Berquist, Stephen Burns, Cláudio Carvalhaes, Jennifer Te Paa Daniel, Lynne St. Clair Darden, Christine J. Hong, Wonhee Anne Joh, HyeRan Kim-Cragg, Boyung Lee, April-faye Tayag Manalang, Loida Yvette Martell, Stephanie Y. Mitchem, Jea Sophia Oh, Nicolas Esteban Panotto, Jeremy Punt, Patrick Reyes, Joerg Rieger, Fernando Segovia, Melinda McGarrah Sharp, Kay Higuera Smith, Jonathan Y. Tan, Mona West, Amos Yong

This series responds to the growing interest in postcolonial studies and reexamines the hegemonic, European-dominated religious systems of the old and new empires. It critically addresses the colonial biases of religions, the academy, and local faith communities, in an effort to make these institutions more polyvocal, receptive, and empowering to global cultures and epistemologies. The series will engage with a variety of hybrid, overlapping, and intersecting definitions of postcolonialism—as a critical discursive practice, as a political and ideological stance concerned with exposing patterns of dominance and hegemony, and as contexts shaped by ongoing colonization and decolonization. Books in the series will also explore the relationship between postcolonial values and religious practice, and the transformation of religious symbols and institutions in postcolonial contexts beyond the academy. The series aims to make high-quality and original research available to the scholarly community. The series welcomes monographs and edited volumes which forge new directions in contextual research across disciplines and explore key contemporary issues. Established scholars as well as new authors will be considered for publication, including scholars "on the margins" whose voices are underrepresented in the academy and in religious discourse. Authors working in subdisciplines of religious studies or theology are encouraged to submit proposals.

Titles in the Series
Colonialism and the Bible: Contemporary Reflections from the Global South, edited by Tat-siong Benny Liew and Fernando F. Segovia
Ecologies of Participation: Agents, Shamans, Mystics, and Diviners, by Zayin Cabot
Feminist Praxis against U.S. Militarism, edited by Nami Kim and Wonhee Anne Joh
Postcolonial Preaching: Creating a Ripple Effect, by HyeRan Kim-Cragg

Postcolonial Preaching

Creating a Ripple Effect

HyeRan Kim-Cragg

Foreword by John McClure
Afterword by Kathy Black

LEXINGTON BOOKS
Lanham • Boulder • New York • London

Published by Lexington Books
An imprint of The Rowman & Littlefield Publishing Group, Inc.
4501 Forbes Boulevard, Suite 200, Lanham, Maryland 20706
www.rowman.com

6 Tinworth Street, London SE11 5AL, United Kingdom

Copyright © 2021 by The Rowman & Littlefield Publishing Group, Inc.

All rights reserved. No part of this book may be reproduced in any form or by any electronic or mechanical means, including information storage and retrieval systems, without written permission from the publisher, except by a reviewer who may quote passages in a review.

British Library Cataloguing in Publication Information Available

Library of Congress Control Number: 2020949339

ISBN 9781793617095 (cloth) | ISBN 9781793617118 (pbk)
ISBN 9781793617101 (epub)

Contents

Foreword		vii
Acknowledgments		ix
Introduction: Why Postcolonial Preaching?		1
1	Rehearsal: Practicing the Realm of God Here and Now but Not Quite Yet	13
2	Imagination: Proclaiming a New World beyond Our Immediate Grasp	29
3	Place: Grappling with Colonial Realities and Locating One's Own Social Location	47
4	Pattern: Vessels to Carry the Living Water	67
5	Language: Becoming a Postcolonial Polyglot with Cultural Linguistic Competency	87
6	Exegesis: Exploring a Postcolonial Contrapuntal Reading for Interpreting Scripture	105
Conclusion: What Next?		123
Afterword		129
Bibliography		131
Index		141
About the Author		149

Foreword

Times have changed. Dreams of a less-divided, more diverse, and more hospitable world are now challenged by global forces of nationalism, racism, and xenophobia. These forces have surged in positions of public leadership, on social media, and in local communities and congregations. In *Postcolonial Preaching: Creating a Ripple Effect* HyeRan Kim-Cragg articulates a clear and realistic homiletical agenda to meet these troubled times. She knows what she is talking about. As a Canadian of Asian descent, she knows only too well how "Asia" as a colonializing construct denies her fullness of place and voice on a daily basis.

I am a white, cis-gendered, North American male, the kind of person who has most to learn from this book. I am inspired by the courage of its author. HyeRan Kim-Cragg is not afraid to confront the difficult issues that consume us these days as preachers who want to speak a gospel of justice. Her vision of the world pushes far beyond the world depicted in mid-twentieth-century Hollywood sitcoms. It is the world as it is today, and as it will be tomorrow—filled with diversity of race, ethnicity, culture, education, gender, sexual orientation, age, economic situation, and ability. It is on behalf of this "spatial plurality" of the Realm of God that she writes. This takes courage in these times. In every aspect, her agenda challenges the insular and individualistic theology that permits and perpetuates the privilege of persons in my demographic.

Although she writes as one committed to social resistance and change, she also writes with striking generosity. Situated within her own multicultural experience and situation, Kim-Cragg writes *with* firsthand experience of immigration, racial and ethnic stereotyping, and patriarchy, yet she writes *from* her commitment to a new and better world. She invites us forward by encouraging a new kind of imagination and new ways to rehearse and live into the Realm of God. It's as if she is an artist and wants to create on canvas a new and better homiletical place for us to inhabit as preachers and teachers of preaching. As I read, I experienced firsthand the ripple effects that accompany her vision of the world. This world has a liberating edge for all of us. None live in God's freedom until all live in God's freedom.

HyeRan Kim-Cragg wants to expand our usual definition of "colonial." She is an intersectional thinker. She knows that preaching is colonized by many intersecting social and political forces. For instance, we cannot assume that a feminist approach to preaching is not simultaneously racist, or that because a homiletical approach is crafted within and in response to a particular racial or ethnic experience it is not simultaneously patriarchal. Her vision of a postcolonial "Kin-dom of God" is one in which "decolonized" has many interlocking aspects. There is great critical wisdom in this, and it suggests a far greater welcome space for preaching to occupy in the next generation.

In each chapter, I experience Professor Kim-Cragg getting down into the dirt with those of us who preach on a regular basis, helping us re-tool our homiletical ways. She is a practical theologian, and she wants preachers to develop new and theologically shaped habits that decolonize their preaching. She gives us not just "hints and helps for better preaching," but encourages an entirely new habitus or "feel for the game" for preaching. In order to make this accessible and workable, she borrows and reinterprets useful categories from performance theory. These new homiletical categories work well for readers like me. They train us how to preach from a new decolonized place, with a new theological vision to rehearse, imagine, shape, articulate, and fully perform when we preach.

At the end of each chapter, Kim-Cragg dons the cap of mentor. She takes the time to carefully craft sermons that demonstrate what she is talking about. Many of us learn by imitation, and these sermons are worth imitating. They are not just the "icing on the cake" for each chapter. They show us the actual ingredients that make a postcolonial sermon what it is—exegetically, theologically, morally, and compositionally. As we see what she does from within her social location, we extrapolate directly into our own situations—learning firsthand what can happen in the pulpit if we harness a genuine postcolonial imagination.

I have renewed hope because of this book, and because of its author. There are fresh winds of God's Spirit blowing in the preaching world today, and it's getting me up, out the door, and into new rippling waters of justice. I know that every reader has their own experience of a book, but I think this last experience might just be one that we all will share together after reading *Postcolonial Preaching: Creating a Ripple Effect.*

John S. McClure
Charles G. Finney Professor of Preaching and Worship
Vanderbilt Divinity School

Acknowledgments

Writing a book is hard work. However, I found writing this book particularly challenging. Part of the reason is that I had to write it as I was transitioning to a new school, Emmanuel College, Toronto. This, of course, meant leaving my previous school that I worked for more than ten years, St. Andrew's College, Saskatoon. This transition was challenging. I did not realize how much the living wide open sky, the wandering prairie rivers, and the dear community of that place had come to mean to me. Moving back to the noisy city and walking streets lined by skyscrapers took some adjustment, even if I am an urban person and enjoys so many wonderful things that this big city offers.

Despite this, I have been truly blessed to come back to the place that was pivotal in my academic journey. As the original meaning of Latin word, "alma mater" implies Emmanuel College has been a "nourishing mother." This school is part of Victoria University of the University of Toronto and is embedded in the Toronto School of Theology. I am grateful for its incredible academic resources: libraries, librarians, colleagues, and brilliant students. I have been intellectually, emotionally, spiritually fed. Their encouraging words, kind gesture, sense of humor, and stimulating conversation, especially with PhD students in my doctoral seminar, basic degree students in my Homiletics and Faith Formation and Christian Education class kept my energy up to complete this book.

As big as this transition was, however, the biggest challenge that I and others faced this past year was the COVID-19 global pandemic. Emmanuel College was closed in mid-March, including all the libraries just when I needed to check all my references. As I write this now at the dawn of September, getting ready for a new semester of 2020–2021, all the libraries in the University of Toronto are still closed.

I would not have been able to complete the book without my family. Isolating with them has been a source of real blessing in the midst of crisis. My partner, David, has been immensely helpful, reading every single word of the manuscript and providing excellent suggestions. My daughter, Hannah, helped me compile the bibliography. My son, Noah, and my mother-in-law, Mary, looked after housework when I had to focus on the book.

I have also had some great colleagues to thank. I am grateful to Kathy Black at Claremont School of Theology who read my manuscript with enthusiasm and made astute comments. She also wrote the succinct and salient Afterword. I am especially thankful for her support taking the time to read this amidst her own transition as her school moved to Oregon. I am also honored to have John McClure write the Foreword. My extended thanks go to Ron Allen, Andrea Bieler, Heather Elkins, Eunjoo Mary Kim, and Lis Valle (in an alphabetical order) who kindly endorsed the book. I give my thanks to Becca Beurer at Lexington Press who worked diligently to make sure to secure peer reviewers despite the challenge with limited staff and stretched responsibilities due to the COVID-19. I thank for the positive and constructive comments of the peer reviewer, which made the book clear and presentable. I also express my gratitude to Michael Gibson, Senior Acquisitions Editor at Lexington, who moved through the final stage of the printing with such energy and graciousness.

Living in the midst of the COVID-19 means that all of us experience incredible stress and fear of uncertainty. I acknowledge that some face much more difficulties than others. The fact that I was able to complete this book means that I am very privileged. COVID-19 has opened up the wounds and the hidden injustices in every sector of society around the world. It is paradoxical that the invisible virus makes injustices of racism, poverty, homelessness, inhumane long-term care facilities, and the plight of undocumented migrants visible. But faith works in the same way, making visible through works of the invisible Spirit, the realm of God on earth here and now!

Introduction

Why Postcolonial Preaching?

The winds of chauvinism are blowing hard around the world at the dawn of the second decade of the second millennia. There are frightening forces at work in our world and within us that are killing us, tearing us apart. Walls are going up around the world to keep people separated from one another. The barriers that are erected allow some to hoard wealth and food in one place and keep it from people in another. Hateful words float in the streets and in our homes. They travel over the internet, dividing people into categories of race, gender, sexual orientation, religion, social class, pronouncing some worthy of respect, and others worthy of disdain. The process of colonization that robbed some of land and language for centuries and which divided people according to such categories continues to rob people of their dignity and lives in the present. This is the context in which we are called to preach the Good News today.

This book confronts, rather than avoids, the harsh winds of 2020, the wind of colonialism, the wind of white supremacy, and the wind of the rhetoric of "building walls." It begins with the premise that to confront these winds is the task of preaching. Today we live in an era, marked by the postcolonial context of migration. This is a complex and dangerous context for many. Most migrants are displaced by force due to war, poverty, and climate change. They flee violence and yet the new places where they arrive are not always safe either. This is why the issues of migration, including the precarious reality of undocumented people, have become everyday news. Those of us living in North America notice that our neighborhood is changing dramatically. I currently live north of Toronto, Canada, in a place that used to be farmlands but was developed as a residential area in the 1980s. This suburb used to be predominantly a white Anglo neighborhood. Now there are large numbers of people from places, such as Syria, Lebanon, Iran, India, China, Korea, and the Philippines, to just name a few. It is normal to hear people talking languages other than English on my daily walk. The local grocery store closest to my home has recently been bought by Chinese businesspeople. The shelves are now stocked with rice instead of bread, fish instead of cheese. The storefront signs along the main road have similarly been changed from English to Arabic, Chinese, or any number of different languages. The people and goods smell different and look different. Churches are not immune to these changes.

This book asks, what does this postcolonial context have to do with preaching? It argues that preaching must attend to the changing demographics of the congregations and their preachers, demographics that bring people face to face with the legacy of a shared colonial past. In short, the book calls for an earnest engagement with postcolonial realities. Preaching as a communicative event always deals with interpersonal dynamics. Yet, despite the many daily interactions that involve differences in language, culture, and national origin, many mainline white middle-class congregations continue to take a monolingual and homogenous culture for granted. Preachers in these congregations, if they are aware of the problem, struggle to address culture, education, social status, language, race, and ethnicity because they have not been given the tools to do so.

Addressing our postcolonial reality from the pulpit requires a practical theological approach. As a discipline, a field of study, practical theology gives priority of lived experiences and attends to concrete realities that need pastoral, prophetic, and ethical attention. Practical theology is not only about application, as if context is detached from abstract knowledge and experience is detached from theory. Practical theology denounces such a binary approach to understanding. Context is integral to, rather than in addition to theological reflection, critical analysis, biblical interpretation, and ethical action, all of which are essential to homiletics. Taking an academic stance, one may find a common thread between practical theology and postcolonial studies as both seek to address, investigate, and respond to current realities through critical reflection.

In fact, the very conversation between postcolonial studies and practical theology has just begun. There has not yet been substantial work dealing with postcolonial studies from a homiletical perspective. The considerable engagement between postcolonial studies and Christian theological disciplines is a relatively recent development, too. One may wonder why this interdisciplinary conversation has taken so long. It may be worthwhile to take a moment to review the process that brought postcolonial scholarship to the attention of homiletics, how the first stone was dropped in the pool of academic knowledge and rippled out to reverberate in scholarship in the field of preaching today.

The person most associated with the beginning of postcolonial studies is Edward Said who in 1978 published *Orientalism*.[1] This book examines how Western writing about colonized people during the period of Western imperial expansion helped to shape the idea of an "Orient" and dehumanize the people affected by colonialism. Works such as Homi Bhabha's *Locations of Culture* published in 1984 follow Said's insights to some extent.[2] Bhabha explored not only the way that the period of colonialism and its ideas continued to shape global interactions but also the way the victims of colonial ideologies and prejudices were subverting the status quo through intriguing processes such as mimicry and hybridity. In 1989, by Bill Ashcroft, Gareth Griffiths, and Helen Tiffin consolidated much of the postcolonial thought developed thus far in *The Empire Writes Back*, establishing postcolonialism as a recognizable and influential theory in the academy.[3]

Kwok Pui-lan, a pioneer postcolonial feminist theologian who I turn to often for insights in this book, has helped us to understand the process through which postcolonial studies have come into conversation with different Christian disciplines.[4] According to her, it was in the mid-1990s that biblical studies made initial contact with postcolonial studies. The two disciplines had a natural affinity. Postcolonial studies were born and developed in the 1970s and 1980s from the discipline of literary criticism, which was concerned with the reading of texts. Biblical studies, also obviously occupied with reading and interpreting texts, found that it had much to learn from postcolonial criticism. R. S. Sugirtharajah was one of the first biblical scholars to vigorously translate postcolonial theories into biblical scholarship.[5] Through biblical studies, then, postcolonial studies were introduced to systematic theology in the 2000s. The work of theologians such as Kwok who had a cross-disciplinary interest in biblical scholarship did much of the work to introduce postcolonial ideas to the theological field.[6]

It was almost a decade later that the ripples of postcolonialism finally reached the disciplines of practical theology. In April 2013, at a meeting of the International Academy of Practical Theology (IAPT) in Toronto with the theme of "Complex Identities in a Shifting World,"[7] postcolonial perspectives emerged as an important area of concern in practical theology. The following year, October 2014, the Center for Practical Theology at the Boston University School of Theology (BU) sponsored a consultation on "Preaching and Postcolonial Theology." Kwok was a keynote speaker for this consultation and clearly pointed out that postcolonial studies as an academic approach was "under-researched" in the area of homiletics.[8] Her address and some initial forays into the subject were published in *Homiletic* subsequently.[9] Shortly after that BU consultation, the neighboring Episcopal Divinity School held a conference on "Challenging the Church: Postcolonial Practice of Ministry," out of which an anthology emerged.[10]

Holding up this rather short trajectory, I present this book. Homiletics engaging postcolonial studies is still in its early stages. Postcolonial studies investigate the multilayered impacts of colonialism. The term "colonialism" refers to the policy or practice of justifying full or partial political control over another country particularly in the modern period, even though I recognize that Empires have existed since the ancient time in different parts of the world. The scope of modern colonial control ranges from occupying a territory militarily and exploiting it economically to settling and repopulating an area to extracting natural and human resources from a territory. The colonial control often involves the use of military force, cultural imperialism, and ideological domination. In this regard, postcolonialism is historical, concerned with the social, political, economic, and cultural conditions of the current world order that are a hangover from the colonial past. Postcolonialism is also heuristic, refusing to remain in the past, a way of analysis involving a critical discursive practice for today and the future by interrogating vicious aspects of modernity and Eurocentric epistemology. That is where postcolonial criticism on the theological terrain gains its pivotal importance because it makes a powerful connection between how God is implicated in the colonial conquest as part of the 3-G, Gun, Gold, and God, triangle. Since the interlocking 3-G aspect of colonialism is tenacious, the discourse of postcolonialism and its decisive action and practice for change must be also intertwined to make a powerful impact. I see the scholarship of postcolonial preaching presented here as one of the first stones to be dropped in the lake of the study of preaching in the hopes that the ripples will expand outward and eventually effect a change in the discipline at every level, contributing to a bigger, stronger, and wider circle of influence in our congregations and in our world.

Facing white supremacy and the colonial legacy of North American society is an urgent task of preaching. What is required is an attitude that will not yield and is endlessly persistent but is nevertheless flexible and able to bend in response to changing situations and contexts. Postcolonial preaching in this sense becomes like a bamboo tree, supple enough to bend but strong enough not to be broken. The postcolonial vision is not iconoclastic and does not seek to erase the past. Rather, like a ripple in a lake, it moves out with reference to certain central events that continue to impact our lives. Postcolonial scholarship examines works that contribute to colonial patterns or fall short of adequately dealing with them. These works are not ignored but held up, critically examined and where possible, used in imagining something new and better. That is why this book takes past scholarship with all its limitations seriously. While the work of homiletics from postcolonial perspectives is novel, the approach to postcolonial preaching proposed here is not filled with everything new. Readers may find many familiar scholarly contributions. While those white and nonwhite scholars who have suffered from colonial violence may be epistemologically privileged for this kind of work, the postcolonial world is marked by ambiguities and fractures, nuances and contradictions, messiness, and porous boundaries. The bottom line is we cannot go back to the precolonial world, the world before colonial conquest took place. But we *can* dream together and work together to create a world, a different world, where colonial wounds are healed and new life springs from a soil rich in honesty and imagination.

I have already introduced the metaphor of the ripples expanding outward from a stone dropped in water. This is a metaphor that I find compelling and which forms a grounding metaphor for this book. Preaching, I maintain, can be effective in addressing postcolonial concerns if it is gentle, but persistent, like small waves emanating from a Gospel truth. These gentle but persistent waves can stir up minds and move hearts with a call to change our way of living and interacting with one another. The book suggests that this ripple effect can be produced and reinforced using six preaching principles that draw on postcolonial insights developed elsewhere: Rehearsal, Imagination, Place, Pattern, Language, and Exegesis.

These principles can be understood as follows. "Rehearsal" of the reign or kin-dom[11] of God is the action of the worship leader that invites the congregation to symbolically enact a community of radical justice and peace. "Imagination" is what the preacher uses to help the congregation conjure a new world in their minds and hearts. "Place" stands for the attention the preacher must pay to their postcolonial context. "Patterns" are critical as they shape the way the Gospel message is conveyed in a sermon. "Language" is a cultural, literary, and rhetorical medium, which preachers need to be conscious of contexts such as global migration in order to reach their audience and avoid reinforcing colonial patterns. "Exegesis" is where the preacher with the congregation wrestles with the scriptural texts and interprets for and from the current postcolonial world.

Imagine that the world is like a lake. The Gospel drops like a pebble into its water, creating a circular pattern of ripples expanding out in all directions. Each ripple is distinct yet connected to the others. Within seconds of the pebble being dropped there are multiple ripples, each one hard to distinguish from the other. None are more or less important. They follow and reinforce one another. In the same way, each of the principles or movements in the RIPPLE pattern reinforces one another. None take precedence over the others. They are simply meant as a way to discern the energy emitted by postcolonial ideas into the process of preaching.

When I wrote *Interdependence*,[12] I envisioned each chapter as a circle layered upon other circles, even though I did not explicitly name this imaginative construct in the book. I organized each chapter as if they were widening circles, the dynamic ideas in each connected through reciprocal relationships with the preceding and following chapters. That is why *Interdependence* begins with examining the self, personhood as the first circle. The first circle of the self is widened as it is seen as part of and mutually dependent on the next circle, family. The family circle is widened as it participates in the church, or other religious community. Then I examined the fourth circle of Christianity and religion as a whole, and then the nation as another circle ever outward and intersecting other circles in the context of migration. The last circle is the planet, the biggest circle you might say, within which all living beings find themselves. I presented the chapters in this way in order to contest the linear and hierarchical western human developmental theory and its separate and individualist notion of the self. Instead, I tried to showcase a relational, communal, and interdependent understanding of human development. Psychologist Urie Bronfenbrenner, examining human development as a process and a result of the interaction with the environment, suggested that a person's life is like expanding circles that join other social circles.[13] I suggested concentric circling as one postcolonial way of imagining practical theology.

Homiletics as a subdiscipline of practical theology may also benefit from this approach. Christian preaching is a social and public act. Its theory and practice seek to cultivate Christian persons within a community that reflects and seeks God's love. My idea of practical theology is about widening concentric circles of life. Expanding on this, my proposal for homiletics is inspired by other homileticians. Don Wardlaw, for example, proposes preaching as a loop of three interlocking circles, all within one all-encompassing circle. These three circles are text, people, and preacher within a wider circle of the cultural context. He writes, "The Word at the preaching moment consists of three key interlocks: the interface of scripture text with preacher; the interrelation of preaching with people; and the interconnection of the people with Scripture. This loop of threefold interplay, all set in and sensitive to the contemporary social context, constitutes the Word-event."[14] Taking up from my own earlier thinking of postcolonial practical theology, and joining in with other scholars, I propose here that postcolonial preaching is a circular multidimensional movement, with the purpose of creating a ripple effect in people's hearts and minds for the sake of the Kin-dom. While the following chapters are organized by six principles, following the spelling of the word, "ripple," the order in which they are presented does not imply a particular logic or sequence other than to suggest that these six are essential elements for postcolonial preaching. However, it can be used as a checklist, ensuring that preacher considers what the essential elements of addressing complex postcolonial contexts are. The important thing is that these categories are meant to be thought of as less mechanical and more organic, less static, and more fluid.

REHEARSAL

Systematic theologian Shannon Craigo-Snell called the church a performance, contesting the view of church narrowly defined as a building, a denomination, or an institution. She writes that the church is where a disciplined performance of relationship with God in Jesus Christ mediated by Scripture and in the hope of the Holy Spirit takes place.[15] Her theology of church enables us to consider preaching as a rehearsal of the ongoing drama of God's salvation. Any theatrical drama needs rehearsal. In a similar vein, the drama of the church also requires rehearsal. Rehearsal for life in God's Kin-dom happens on Sunday morning and elsewhere. The sermon is a part of that rehearsal. But rehearsing God's drama in our lives takes place at other times as well. Rehearsal of the realm of God may occur during a choir practice, getting ready for Eucharist, weekday committee meetings, or the Bible study on weekdays. It may also take place in non-church contexts.

Preaching proclaims the surprising grace of the God who heals and reconciles us into a new humanity and restores the entire creation to its wholeness. Sunday worship is a sign to the world that, even if only momentarily, a new world has already dawned. Preaching becomes a rehearsal to the new social reality. This transient, transcendent, and transcending proclamation ushers in an eschatological vision. Preaching eschatologically means that we expose the enslaving and oppressive realities of our society today and in the past. Preaching exposes the troubles we see and sins we have committed without sugarcoating them. But preaching does not stop at simply unveiling the sinful reality, even if such is a crucial component of preaching. Postcolonial preaching attempts to move beyond naming the broken reality and offers a glimpse of the imagined world; the world as God intends it to be. This is an important aspect of rehearsal in preaching.

IMAGINATION

Imagination is about venturing to the very edge of humanizing possibilities. Rehearsal and imagination are closely related. In the words of biblical scholar Walter Brueggemann, the work of imagination is to "picture, portray, receive and practice the world in ways other than it appears to be at first glance when seen through a dominant, habitual, unexamined lens."[16] Imagination in this sense is a form of rehearsal. To Justo Gonzalez, the seasoned historian who wrote preaching books, preaching imagination is a countercultural act because preaching has "cut across the grain of the dominant culture and dared to proclaim a reality that that culture tended to suppress."[17] Postcolonial theologian Kwok Pui-lan similarly contends that imagination serves as a challenge to the status quo, including the assumptions of the colonial past. She writes, "Postcolonial imagination refers to . . . a process of disengagement from the whole colonial syndrome." This process necessarily involves examining "how the colonial systems of knowledge cast their impact, long after the colonizers are gone."[18]

PLACE

Postcolonial preaching regards place as an essential component of the preaching act. Here place connotes several dimensions. First, place refers to the context in which preaching happens. Addressing this particularity of place brings forth the importance of the contextual analysis of the current world for preaching. This includes, for example, the historical nature of place as in the place where conquest took place. Modern European colonialism shaped and continues to shape the place of preaching in North America and the entire world today. An interrogation of this history needs to happen in order for preaching to be able to address the ongoing social consequences of colonialism. Key theoretical concepts deriving from postcolonial scholarship such as orientalism, representation, mimicry, and trickster are useful for locating and identifying the place of preaching in its historical context.

Second, at a microlevel, the place of preaching refers to the pulpit. The pulpit is a liturgical object, which was used as the Christian symbol reinforcing preaching authority, and in the colonial context, this also means white male authority. The pulpit is not unrelated to colonial expansion and the process of civilizing mission. The pulpit also points to the social location of the preacher and that of the congregation. Preachers should consciously know how their social locations, in terms of race, ethnicity, class, sexual orientation, gender identity, ability, and language, influence their biblical interpretation, their theology, their pastoral awareness, and their homiletical methodologies.[19]

The discourse on the pulpit, its location, and its use, is never simple. There is certainly no easy or clear position that everyone can agree on. Those racialized women who preferred to use the pulpit for preaching argued that the pulpit is a symbol of preaching authority and that using it compensates for their marginal identities of their nonwhite female bodies. Given that the pulpit is still a white man's place, it is important to claim it as a woman's as well as a racialized place by preaching from that very location as a postcolonial feminist practice of agency.[20]

Place and identity go hand in hand in postcolonial theory. The changing landscapes of migration are a critical contemporary context of preaching. This emerging context urges preachers to study and examine "not only how and what to preach but also where and therefore with whom to preach."[21] Locating a preaching place situated in the complex and changing world of the twenty-first century involves addressing the migration and postcolonial context.

PATTERN

Similar to the first and the second RIPPLE effects of Rehearsal and Imagination, Place and Pattern, the third and the fourth principles, are also interrelated and complimentary to each other. On the North American continent, the colonial place of preaching was shaped by the arrival of the Puritans from England. Looking for appropriate preaching patterns is like seeking a proper vessel to carry the water of the Gospel and deliver it to who those who need it. Any sermonic pattern cannot be separated from its content, the message. Hence, I will review various patterns, including deductive and expository ones as well as inductive, and narrative patterns. This review also includes the comparison of prevalent patterns in feminist and Asian, African, and Latinx preaching. A postcolonial preaching pattern incorporates other patterns.

LANGUAGE

As a fifth component of the RIPPLE effect, language, its diversity, and its intercultural dynamics, is essential for overcoming the legacy of colonialism and reflecting current migration realities. In the denomination to which I belong, the United Church of Canada, the rate of ordained preachers who are admitted from other countries in recent years is almost equal to the number of locally trained preachers who are ordained from within to serve the congregations of the denomination. I have had the privilege of teaching a number of these preachers from other countries. Most of them are nonwhite and speak more than one language or speak English with a non-normative accent. Equipping recent immigrant preachers, as well as North American born preachers, with an appreciation of their place within an intercultural, multilinguistic context is a growing need that those of us who either teach homiletics or preach regularly must attend to.

The language of preaching, spoken or sign language, points to the core vocational identity of the preacher and the corporate identity of the church.[22]

If language is not merely a tool to describe a past or current reality but also a means to create a future reality—an alternative, an anticipated Kin-dom of God—then whose language is represented in preaching is a choice that will shape the church and the world in which we want to live. That is why this book pays special attention to language, its power, its multiple meanings, both positive and negative, as well as the embodied, visual, nonverbal, and animated linguistic functions in preaching. To speak of these multifaceted languages, we must equip ourselves to become polyglot as we, preachers and homileticians, gain intercultural and linguistic competency adequately responsive to postcolonial migration contexts. Addressing complicated postcolonial migration realities is not merely an additional justice issue but should be considered as a core part of homiletics.

EXEGESIS

The discussion of language leads finally to the sixth component of the RIPPLE effect: exegesis. The final chapter argues that effective scriptural exegesis for preaching cannot happen if the reader/preacher does not understand and reflect upon the colonial realities embedded in the Bible. Hence, noting the palpable silence on the colonial reality in most of the exegetical literature, I argue for the contrapuntal strategy first developed by Edward Said,[23] which is integral to postcolonial interpretations of the Bible. This particular reading strategy allows preachers to zoom in on the colonial experiences of people, otherwise hidden and unspoken in the Bible. Biblical texts and the people they describe were very much beholden to colonial realities of their time.

This book attempts to elaborate and expand upon each of the above components of the RIPPLE effect and thereby expand our awareness of the call to postcolonial preaching. It does so in the conviction that postcolonial preaching can provide a vision, an alternative, as a way of holding a creative tension in contradiction, to the forces of neocolonialism, carrying a different energy, and to offering a glimpse of the divine movement towards the Kin-dom of God. The lofty and humble task of postcolonial preaching will, it is hoped, contribute to the church's witness to God's love in the face the deadly winds of our time, as it is inbreathed by the life-giving breath of the Holy Spirit, the *Ruach* of God's creative possibility for all people and creation.

NOTES

1. Edward Said, *Orientalism* (New York: Knopf, 1978).
2. Homi Bhabha, *The Location of Culture* (New York: Routledge, 1994).

3. Bill Ashcroft et al., *The Empire Writes Back: Theory and Practice in Post-Colonial Literature* (New York: Routledge), 1989.

4. Kwok Pui-Lan, *Discovering the Bible in a Non-Biblical World* (Maryknoll: Orbis, 1995); *Postcolonial Imagination and Feminist Theology* (Louisville: Westminster/John Knox, 2005).

5. R. S. Sugirtharajah, ed., *Voices from the Margins: Interpreting the Bible in the Third World* (London: SPCK, 1995); *The Postcolonial Bible* (Sheffield: Sheffield Academic Press, 1998); *The Bible and the Third World: Postcolonial Encounters* (Cambridge: Cambridge University Press, 2001).

6. Catherine Keller, Michael Nausner, and Mayra Rivera, eds., *Postcolonial Theologies: Divinity and Empire* (St. Louis, MO: Chalice Press, 2004); Wonhee Anne Joh, *Heart of the Cross: A Postcolonial Christology* (Louisville: Westminster John Knox, 2006), Mayra Rivera, *The Touch of Transcendence: A Postcolonial Theology of God* (Louisville: Westminster John Knox, 2007).

7. Pamela Couture, Robert Mager, Pamela McCarroll, and Natalie Wigg-Stevenson, eds., *Complex Identities in a Shifting World: Practical Theological Perspectives* (Zurich: LIT, 2015).

8. Kwok Pui-lan, "Epilogue," in *Postcolonial Practice of Ministry: Leadership, Liturgy, and Interfaith Engagement*, ed. Kwok Pui-lan and Stephen Burns (Lanham: Lexington, 2016), 215.

9. *Homiletic* 40:1 (2015): 3–62. Around that time, Sarah Travis's book has been out based on her doctoral dissertation: *Decolonizing Preaching: The Pulpit as Postcolonial Space* (Eugene: Cascade, 2014). Travis critically examines how colonial discourse is violent in terms of destroying human relationships. Highlighting her Trinitarian theology, she utilizes postcolonial insights and suggests how preaching can be a means and a remedy for decolonizing the pulpit. My book does not engage the Trinity extensively but shares similar views in terms of preaching as a relational event.

10. Kwok Pui-lan, and Stephen Burns, eds., *Postcolonial Practice of Ministry: Leadership, Liturgy, and Interfaith Engagement* (Lanham: Lexington, 2016).

11. This term "'kin-dom of God" was coined by Ada Maria Isasi-Diaz in "Solidarity: Love of the Neighbor in 1980s," in *Life Every Voice: Constructing Christian Theologies from the Underside*, ed. Susan Brooks Thistlethwaite, and Mary Potter Engel (San Francisco: Harper and Row, 1990), 31–40. I will use kin-dom, reign, and realm interchangeably throughout the book.

12. HyeRan Kim-Cragg, *Interdependence: A Postcolonial Practical Theology* (Eugene: Pickwick, 2018).

13. Urie Bronfenbrenner, *The Ecology of Human Development: Experiment by Nature and Design* (Cambridge: Harvard University Press, 1979).

14. Don M. Wardlaw, "Preaching as the Interface of Two Social Worlds: The Congregation as Corporate Agent in the Act of Preaching," in *Preaching as a Social Act: Theology and Practice*, ed. Arthur Van Seters (Abingdon: Nashville, 1988), 63.

15. Shannon Craigo-Snell, *The Empty Church: Theology, Theatre and Embodied of Hope* (Oxford University Press, 2011), 5.

16. Walter Brueggemann, *Text under Negotiation: The Bible and Postmodern Imagination* (Minneapolis: Fortress, 1993), 13.

17. Justo Gonzalez, "Minority Preaching in a Postmodern Age," in *Sharing Heaven's Music: The Heart of Christian Preaching: Essays in Honor of James Earl Massey*, ed. Barry L. Callen (Nashville: Abingdon Press, 1995), 190.

18. Kwok Pui-lan, *Postcolonial Imagination and Feminist Theology* (Louisville: Westminster John Knox, 2005), 2–3.

19. HyeRan Kim-Cragg, "Unfinished and Unfolding Tasks of Preaching: Interdisciplinary, Intercultural, and Interreligious Approaches in the Postcolonial Context of Migration," *Homiletic* 44:2 (2019): 4.

20. HyeRan Kim-Cragg, "Probing the Pulpit: Postcolonial Feminist Perspectives," *Liturgy* 34 (2019): 22–30.

21. Yohan Go, David S. Jacobsen, and Duse Lee, "Making New Spaces in Between: A Post-Reflective Essay Weaving Postcolonial Threads into North American Homiletics," *Homiletic* 40:1 (2015): 56.

22. Paul Scott Wilson, *God Sense: Reading the Bible for Preaching* (Nashville: Abingdon, 2001).

23. Edward Said, *Culture and Imperialism* (New York: Knopf, 1993).

Chapter 1

Rehearsal

Practicing the Realm of God Here and Now but Not Quite Yet

> *But seek first the kingdom (Basileia) of God and God's righteousness, and all these things will be given to you as well.*
>
> —Matt. 6:33, NRSV

As the first principle of the ripple effect, this chapter considers preaching as rehearsal. Preaching as rehearsal deals with twofold meanings: on one hand, preaching as rehearsal is used to underscore the importance of practice, namely, rehearsal for the act of preaching itself. On the other hand, preaching as rehearsal points to what the community of faith does, in anticipation of the coming realm of God. Preaching as a rehearsal of the realm of God anticipates a *Kairos* moment and engages a foretaste of the new reality. Postcolonial preaching as rehearsal helps to expound the goal of preaching as a kind of anticipation of the realm of God in a *Kairos* sense.

PREACHING AS PRACTICE

The emphasis on the Christian practice of preaching generated interest among homiletical scholars in the 1980s. The work of the Task Force on Pedagogy and Preaching in the Academy of Homiletics released in 1983 at a meeting in Toronto was issued by eight teachers of preaching who examined how preaching can be effectively learned. They met together over two years and deepened the connection between pedagogy and preaching.[1] More recently, the interest in learning and teaching preaching was renewed by some teachers of preaching who highlighted practice as an organizing framework in homiletics. This time the focus was on practice, in addition to learning and teaching. Here, practice is defined as "a constellation of actions that people have performed over time that are common, meaningful, strategic and purposeful."[2] This definition is influenced by a broader definition of practice as "a living, developing practice," what Christians "do together over time to address fundamental human needs in response to and in the light of God's active presence in the world."[3]

Preaching is one of the oldest Christian practices. Early Church communities were formed and grew as they practiced weekly gatherings; devoted themselves to teaching and learning, hearing, and witnessing to the gospel; prayed and shared meals together; and went out to attend the sick and serve those in need (Acts 2:37–47). These basic Christian practices have lasted over two millennia and can be boiled down to five essential elements: gathering/fellowship (*Koinonia*), hearing/witnessing (*Kerygma*), teaching and learning (*Didache*), praying/sharing meals (*Leiturgia*), and service/outreach (*Diakonia*).[4] These five elements, of course, cannot be entirely separated from one another. There is no preaching when people do not gather, for example. Sharing the good news as *Kerygma* is not as effective without the accompanying practice of sharing meals as an expression of thanksgiving to God (*Eucharist*). Preaching is not complete unless and until service (*Diakonia*) outside the church has begun. Preaching in the congregation ends so that service in the world can start. These five essential Christian practices contributed to forming what we now call liturgy. The so-called liturgical *Ordo*,[5] "Gathering, Word, Thanksgiving, and Sending Forth," was established and observed in many, albeit not all, churches in the 1990s.[6] The second movement of word includes the ancient churches' *Kerygma* and *Didache*. It has taken the form of what we now call preaching, which often involves teaching and learning, as well as hearing and witnessing to the Gospel.

REHEARSAL AS PRACTICE

The term "rehearsal" in homiletics and liturgical theology is borrowed from theater studies. Theater studies by its nature are interdisciplinary as it encompasses and crosses into such disciplines as hermeneutics, semiotics, and performativity, to just name a new. Homiletics, too, has been indebted to these disciplines since they similarly deal with interpreting texts, probing meanings embedded in signs and metaphors, and embodied communication. To further adopt the notion of rehearsal from theater studies for use in a study of preaching is, therefore, not a surprise, but a natural fit. Homiletician Anna Carter Florence recalls her first encounter with theater studies during her undergraduate work, and her discovery of the significance of the practice in the learning of theory.[7] The work of rehearsing as a way of understanding a text is essential in theater studies. This symbiosis between theory and practice is key to understanding rehearsal. Rehearsal is an activity for public presentation in the performing arts. It occurs as preparation for a performance in music, theater, dance, opera, and film production. Rehearsal is a form of practice, which requires adequate preparation and precise coordination. Rehearsal also refers to collective activities undertaken by a group of people.

These different aspects of rehearsal offer insights that are directly related to preaching. First, rehearsal stresses the importance of practice as a discipline that ensures a quality of performance and excellence. Preachers, too, need to practice their sermons. Preaching needs rehearsal. Secondly, rehearsal underscores the public dimension. Rehearsal of the sermon is done with the congregation in mind. In the same way plays are for an audience, preaching is a public performance intended for the benefit of the people; it is not the private hobby of the preacher pursuing personal excellence in something, even if personal and public objectives are not mutually exclusive. Thirdly, rehearsal involves a community in its execution. In the same way, preaching aims to empower the whole people of God and involves people in sermon preparation and the preaching act. The ways the congregation is engaged in the sermon can vary. John McClure suggests collaborative brainstorming with others in the congregation as a technique the preacher can employ as a way to engage the congregation in the preparation of sermons.[8] Florence provides five tools for rehearsing scripture, which also require the participation of a group.[9] Finally, rehearsal is physical. Preaching uses human bodies, physical spaces, and symbolic objects as a way of connecting with an audience. These different notions of preaching that transgress the ideal of the solo preacher who delivers a disembodied word from a position of authority remote from the congregation are, as such, postcolonial.

PREACHING AS REHEARSAL OF THE REALM OF GOD

The idea that worship is a rehearsal of the realm of God is one that was developed by liturgical theologian John Burkhart. According to Burkhart, "The participants in the rehearsal—given enough time and space for tryouts and rehearsals, grouping and growing, learning their lines and forgetting them, being prompted and remembering again . . . or even sitting offstage for a while to view the whole scene . . . and, even if for a few moments, may find themselves transformed . . . . In this sense, gatherings for worship are dress rehearsals of life lived by the grace of God."[10] A decade later, Don Saliers took up the theatrical metaphor of rehearsal to discuss liturgical theology. To him, becoming Christian is to be "taken into the dramatic narrative of Jesus Christ" through the liturgy.[11] Christians achieve a foretaste of the realm of

God by playing parts in the theater of God's drama. Gathered as a repertory church, Christian identity is shaped by and found in rehearing the text and engaging with the divine living script. Christians have developed repetitive liturgical patterns that have endured for centuries. What is more, these liturgical patterns play out beyond the assigned time of liturgical gathering. Christians are actors in the drama of God. It is impossible to be a simple bystander and not be involved in the divine drama. Being actors in the theater of God's world also includes being "spectators." Shannon Craig-Snell points out that "spectator" might better be thought of as "spect-actor" in Christian drama. Understood as both see and act, this term points out the role of spectator in a more active sense. Christian preachers are spectators as they both see and act as witnesses to the Gospel.[12] Congregations are also spectators who both see and act rather than merely sit and watch from the pew, because they play an active role in the rehearsal, and even in preaching. Preaching as a rehearsal of the realm of God is to see and act God's love for the world and embody humanity's hope in God throughout ages.

The Christian life as a rehearsal of the realm of God points to an eschatological dimension of the act of preaching. Here "realm" is a translation of the Greek word *basileia* in *Basileia tou Teou* (The realm of God). This word appears more than 100 times in the New Testament. It is mentioned in almost every parable in the synoptic Gospels of Matthew, Mark, and Luke. While there is no perfect translation of *basileia* in English, many versions of the Bible translate it as *Kingdom* as in the case of the New Revised Standard Version (NRSV). Some homileticians have translated it as "realm."[13] Some liturgical theologians have translated it as "kin-dom" rather than kingdom, trying to overcome the idea of a masculine monarchy.[14] The translation of *basileia* as a kin-dom derived from the concept of kinship is helpful because it underscores that the realm of God is not a territory or a building or a nation. Rather it points to relationships as moving and changing, practiced and lived in justice, equity, and peace.[15] When one of the goals of preaching is to seek the realm of God it makes sense to view this realm as a network of relationships.

The view of preaching as a rehearsal of the realm of God stresses the importance of the formation of Christian identity. Christians are made and not born.[16] Christians embody their faith not only in words but also in deeds (James 1:22). By our fruit we are identified as followers of Jesus (Matt. 12:33). Christians believe that when we love one another, we experience God and feel that God lives in us (1 John 4:12). By our living example through their corporate practice, people may experience the presence of God. In a sacramental sense, *basileia* is shared, tasted, seen, and practiced. Preaching as a rehearsal of the realm of God is built as a corporate muscle memory, as the ecclesial body remembers this God through the practice of tasting and seeing, hearing and speaking, touching and caring, and smelling and moving regularly. These various sensory and physical experiences of the realm of God as a practice of the kinship cannot be known unless community in relationships practices faith regularly.

POSTCOLONIAL PREACHING AS A REHEARSAL OF SPATIAL PLURALITY

The realm of God (*basileia*) that Jesus preached is puzzling, far from being clear. On one hand, he seems to refer it to a time, as "the time is fulfilled and the kingdom of God has come near" (Mark 1:14). On the other hand, Jesus seems to indicate a place, when he gave a parable of the realm of God as a mustard seed that "became a tree and the birds of the air made nests in its branches" (Luke 13: 19). Where is the realm of God? When does it come? Is the realm of God a time or a space? Or does it encompass both? If *basileia* includes both, we may claim the intricate relationship between time and the space of the realm of God. Preaching is about proclaiming the hope for the future that is unfolding into the present moments. This is what it means when we speak of preaching as a rehearsal of the realm of God. Tom Long strongly suggests that preachers must lead the congregation to hear the Gospel with "a genuine readiness" and "an air of expectancy."[17] It is critical to nurture an anticipation of the realm of God.

Anticipation and expectation are also connected to the sermon preparation and delivery. Sometimes preparation involves active practice and development of ideas. Other times, however, it is more of a passive process or, better yet, a process of active waiting akin to waiting for an anticipated event like a graduation or a job interview. There is a buildup of energy akin to the way water reaches the boiling point. As the energy builds, there comes a moment when the water begins to transform itself into something else. A similar buildup of feelings and "aha moments" must take place in order for a sermon to reach its *Kairos* moment. Without the rehearsal of anticipation with patience and perseverance, as well as the application of energy, the transformation of water to steam will not happen. There is no Christmas without Advent, and Advent involves the faithful practice of active waiting.[18]

Postcolonial theory has a lot to contribute to a discussion of the Christian eschaton. In postcolonial theory, time and space are enmeshed in the notion of spatial plurality rather than a linear temporality. This approach seeks to counter the colonial prioritization of time over space, which orders the world in a way that deliberately privileges colonial powers. A postcolonial epistemology of "spatial plurality"[19] finds a kindred spirit in the Christian vision of a realm of God, as a paradoxical, nonlinear, and non-dualistic concept; a reality that is here and now but not quite yet. The notion of the realm of God distinguishes *Kairos* from *chronos*.

Postcolonial preaching as a rehearsal of the realm of God contests colonial histories (time) and challenges the colonial legacy, which divides space into areas of "haves" and "have-nots." Colonial power tends to emphasize the past (origin, the place of birth, original authorship and original meaning or intention of the original composition) as a way of undermining the present reality (contemporary readers and current issues). The prioritization of the past works to shore up its claim to authority over the colonized and deprived demands for justice by the same. Yet, fragments of history contain stories of human agency that call into question this authority and provide a glimpse of a more just future.

This is where Paul Ricoeur's interdisciplinary theory of the hermeneutics of meaning is helpful because it highlights the intertwined nature of time and space in interpreting scripture for preaching. Ricoeur suggests a threefold hermeneutical movement beginning with what he terms the first naiveté. In this movement, the preacher and the community see the world of the text in a non-critical way. They try to see the world on the terms implied by the text.[20] Ricoeur's hermeneutical contribution may bear a fruitful insight when we approach preaching as the rehearsal of the realm of God. The world behind the text matters (the first naiveté) as much as the questions that emerge from the text (critical reflection). The world before the readers today anticipates something new, a new world, the reign of God (the second naiveté). For Ricoeur, the present reality (the world before the readers) understood as both a particular time and a particular place is profoundly affected by memories of the past (the world behind the text) as well as by the capacity to imagine the future.[21]

Ron Allen features Pablo Jiménez's sermon as a sample utilizing Ricoeur's hermeneutics where he examines the meaning of partnership in Phil. 1:1–6. In the first movement, the notion of partnership is presented as it has been understood by the community in Philippi. This first movement is followed by the critical reflection on how such biblical partnership affected the powerful and the powerless United States. The third movement goes back to the text as the second naiveté with a renewed understanding of partnership based on equity as subversive partnership where corporate ladder is dismantled.[22] In this movement, the reading is no longer naïve but is willing to suspend certain critical questions in a way that allows different and new insights to emerge. The text does not look the same as it did in the first movement. The reading may realize that the meaning of the text might not necessarily lie in the intentions of the authors (biblical authors included) or the ancient audience of the past only but in the minds and hearts of the readers who look at the text today. A new and different meaning can be drawn and re-actualized by the readers who have no choice but to consider their particular context and their worldly reality when they engage the ancient biblical text. The reality of the text before the readers is as valid as the meaning behind the text. The interaction between these two, behind and before, past and present, generates a new meaning.

That is why a reader-response reading as a preaching practice may be crucially important to a postcolonial homiletical rehearsal. This hermeneutical method helps preachers as the listener and the interpreter of the text proclaim the realm of God that is happening before our present place and behind our past time.[23] As far as reader as human agency is concerned, reader-response exegesis prioritizes the social location of the reader who engages in proclaiming a rehearsal of the realm of God as the promise of the future, which is rooted in the past and entangled with the present in spatial particularity and plurality.

The social location of the preacher as a key identity marker will be discussed more extensively in chapter 3 on place. But it is worth pondering the importance of the identity of the preacher here, as far as problematizing the linear order of time in constructing identity is concerned. Identity as a construction of one's history and experience poses a problem when it is predominantly and narrowly determined by one's past. Identity is understood as "the need for certainty, group solidarity and a sense of communal belonging."[24] This becomes a problem when identity markers become a weapon to exclude a minoritized group and normalize a dominant group. The identities of ethnicity and nationality become unstable when some groups' identities are constructed following the linear notion of time. Identity of the preacher matters as much as the identity of the congregation matters. Identity shapes everything that involves preaching. The way we read the text, the way we read the world, the way we minister to and with our congregation, the way we select sermon illustrations, and the list goes on. Let us say, you are a second-generation US-born preacher. You are ethnically Korean, and you don't hold any passport other than one from the United States. Yet, your origin emerging from the linear notion of time based on your ancestry supersedes your belonging in the space called the United States. Your ethnic origin cannot be erased, and it becomes a determining factor of your identity. Even if you have never put your foot in Korea or do not speak the language, you are seen as Korean in the United States. That is why you have been asked, "Where are you from?" with a subsequently implied question of "When are you going back?" The comment made by the US president Donald Trump who told four congresswomen to "go back to where you came from" reveals this problem of identity politics based on the linear notion of time coupled with racial hierarchy.[25] The so-called border problems, captured by the rhetoric, "build the walls" shouted by those European white settlers expose this unwarranted entitlement as if the place belongs to them because "they were here before you," following the linear progress of time. This is doubly problematic, however. There were indigenous people before these white Europeans came. In many cases, this colonial settlement process was far from being peaceful. For indigenous people, this settlement process for the most part is a stealing process rather than a shared process. The settlement process based on colonial capitalism and anthropocentrism was often carried out by force at the expense of indigenous people and all creatures who cohabited on this land now called North America for millennia.

Preaching as a rehearsal of the realm of God is to practice this cohabitation as we strive for an interdependent and cultivate mutually life-giving kin-relationships. In this regard, preaching is not just a practice on Sunday morning however central it is. It is also a daily practice at home and at work. For preaching that involves shaping faith and shaping practices of people is a way of life.[26] Preaching is a public theological practice that takes the whole world as its preaching space.

This posture of worldly cohabitation suggests a different Christian practice of reading the text and preaching. For instance, with this posture, the presumed traditional expectation of order, as a linear pattern to craft a sermon may be shaken. A typical message of the sermon may be interrupted, precisely through bringing together unexpected elements in the preaching event that arise from the current present realities. Anticipation of postcolonial realities as a rehearsal of the realm of God contributes to alternative perceptions of reality. David Power argues that finding these elements in biblical texts is not difficult. There are plenty of references in the Bible, which can be used as homiletical resources. For example, most parables of Jesus contain surprises and unconventional wisdom. Eschatological visions as a rehearsal of the realm of God, anticipating a new world presented in the Bible shine through the songs of Miriam, Hannah, and Mary, as well as the prophecy of Zachariah as forms of discourse that disrupt and disorient the presumed world of order and the ordering of time.[27]

Walter Brueggemann argues that this is most obvious in prophetic preaching for the goal of preaching is to form an alternative community. Here preaching presses hard on the idea of the "prophetic imagination"[28] anchored in the just seeking relationships of the realm of God.

If the Gospel is understood as a coin, it has two sides. On one side, preaching the Gospel is about proclaiming God's unconditional love (God's mercy and compassion). On the other side, it is about calling for justice. Rehearsing the realm of God as a goal of postcolonial preaching addresses both. Preaching is to rehearse the unconditional love of God and to rehearse God's call for justice as we seek to bring the realm of God on earth. Here rehearsal includes the practice of a sermon in and out of the pulpit. But it also includes a preparation and a dedicated discipline of participating in the kin-dom of God in worship and in our daily lives.

PREACHING THE REHEARSAL OF THE REALM OF GOD: A SACRAMENTAL APPROACH

We have already alluded to the connection between preaching and the liturgy at the beginning of the chapter. Sharing the Good News as a proclamatory rehearsal of the realm of God can be enhanced by the sacramental practice of sharing meals. The Eucharist is central to the proclamatory rehearsal.[29] One of the major purposes of participating in the Eucharist is to literally taste and see that God is good (Ps. 34:8). The sacrament of the Eucharist is the physical and corporate celebration of God's self-giving love. This liturgical act affirms God's goodness. It embodies God's abundant blessing. The Eucharistic practice enables those who participate in it to experience the realm of God. It also reflects the profound meaning involved in the ordinary practice of sharing meals. Breaking bread is an expression for Christians of God's desire for the entire creation of a community where life is shared.

To lift up the mutually affirming actions of preaching and Eucharistic celebration is to critique the unhelpful division of Word and Table in our liturgical history. The division is tenacious. Protestant churches continue to overemphasize the role of preaching at the expense of the Eucharistic celebration, while non-Protestant Churches have not adequately paid attention to the importance of preaching in liturgy but remain focused on the Eucharist to the exclusion of the other. This dichotomy still serves as the background for the tug of war in our worship services today. But the dichotomy between the Word and Table is false. Until and unless both are integrated in holistic and faithful ways in worship, preaching a rehearsal of the kin-dom of God may end up being lip service to an effectively unattainable reality. Hence, it is imperative to engage in a self-critical examination of the theology and practice of the Word (preaching) and Table (Eucharist). One of the aims of this self-critique includes humility. French Catholic theologian Yves Congar humbly acknowledged the other side of the debate when he said, "I could quote a whole series of ancient texts, all saying more or less that if in one country Mass was celebrated for thirty years without preaching, and in another there was preaching for thirty years without the Mass, the people would be more Christian in the country where there was preaching."[30] From the Protestant side can we imagine the cost to our communities of faith when we ignore the Eucharist in worship? How can Protestants be open to learn from Roman Catholicism and other traditions whose whole liturgical practices are conducive and integral to preaching? Claudio Carvalhaes as a

Reformed scholar draws a correlation between the preacher and the whole of the liturgy, lifting up the work of Charles Rice, who said, "The preacher, while always called to careful exegesis and disciplined, imaginative use of language, need not stand in a spotlight or carry the entire weight of worship."[31] It is essential to see "the preached word and the sacramental word to be of whole cloth."[32] The Second Vatican Council began to mend this torn cloth from the Roman Catholic side in the 1960s. It is not a radical or heretical thought any longer that both the Word and Table must be balanced in worship. I would argue, however, that it has not yet been ingrained in our congregational practices to the degree that it is part of our muscle memory. The unhelpful practices have yet to be unlearned and unused muscles have yet to be adequately exercised.

The sacramental integration of Word and Table is also an important aspect of postcolonial preaching because sacramentality points to our embodied nature as creatures of God within a creation with which we are intimately connected. A creation centered approach to preaching helps to ground us in the urgent concern of the Anthropocene age when environmental exploitation and the consumption of fossil fuels threaten our very existence. Postcolonial theologians seek to articulate "planetary loves,"[33] humbly acknowledging that humans are only a small species, rather than the center of the universe. This cosmological view acknowledges that God intends the world for all its creatures. Preaching, therefore, must not merely strive to proclaim "a dwelling place of all of the people"[34] but must seek the right relationship with the entire creation.

The following sermon serves as an example of a sermon as a rehearsal of the Kin-dom of God. Note especially how it expounds the meaning of *basileia* in the search for a home and the already/not yet quality of a place of comfort and safety. The sermon features a common experience in the postcolonial world: the experience of migration and displacement. Although the preacher of this sermon does not speak with firsthand experience of some of the more desperate and tragic aspects of migration in the twenty-first century, the sermon nonetheless addresses the important theme of leaving home to find another home, a place that one can belong to. There is furthermore an eschatological expectation in this movement, which resonates with postcolonial concerns—concerns that are specifically foregrounded in the opening lines.

SERMON EXAMPLE

"Basileia and Bethlehem"
   Ruth 1: 1–7; Matt. 6:25–33

"Stop worrying, over questions such as What to eat? What to drink? Or what are we to wear? Those without faith are always running after these things."

This is what Jesus said.

Stop worrying, really?

Nearly half of the world's population—more than 3 billion people—barely survive each day. More than 1.3 billion among them live in extreme poverty and the majority of them are children worldwide. According to UNICEF, 22,000 children die each day due to poverty. They die because they do not have enough to eat.

Stop worrying, really?

University of Saskatchewan Ecumenical Chaplaincy office decided to serve breakfast for students on the campus a few years ago. The office traditionally used to serve supper, followed by a Bible study, which drew five to ten people regularly. The chaplain wondered what if we serve breakfast instead. Can this change of time attract more students? There was a risk. There is always a risk trying new things that go against the tradition, the way we have always done things. With faith, he lined up several churches, Anglican, Presbyterian, and United, who would provide food and promoted the breakfast programme. It grew ten to twenty, then twenty to forty. It grew from once a day a week to twice a week. The chaplain began to learn that there are students who are too poor to eat three meals a day. Some of the students who came for the breakfast would go hungry without this meal.

Stop worrying, really?

The Gospel text in Matthew we heard today seems incredible, unreasonable, and even unfair. "Don't worry about tomorrow?" How can we not worry about what to eat in the world we live in? Wasn't Jesus asking too much of our faith in God? Or is Jesus asking too little? Don't worry? Will everything really be fine if we don't worry about it? Will everything be taken care of? If we are hungry, I'm sure Jesus is not telling us to lie down under an apple tree until an apple falls into our hand. Then what is he saying?

If we listen to Jesus's sermon only until verse 32, and stop right there, we will conclude with the singer Bobby McFerrin that life's best philosophy is "don't worry; be happy." But I think that to get at what Jesus really means we have to listen a little further, right until the last verse of the sermon, verse 33. "Seek ye first the Kingdom of God and God's righteousness and all these things shall be added unto you" (NRSV). This is an important verse of scripture that we have been singing for many years to a beautiful and well-known tune. I chose not to include verse 34, "So do not worry about tomorrow, for tomorrow will bring worries of its own. Today's trouble is enough for today" even though a lectionary includes this verse. One commentary suggests that this verse was added onto the original source. I agree with the commentary's given reason that it was not included in the Lukan version of this sermon that shares the same original source.

But, more than that, the reason I chose to exclude the verse from what I regard as the true Sermon on the Mount is that it contradicts verse 33. I wonder if omitting this verse is a correct reading of the Bible, especially when we look at chapter 6 as a whole. This is a chapter where the prayer that Jesus taught us to pray appears. This prayer includes an acknowledgment that the Kingdom of God is to come, and that God's will is to be done on earth. It also asks for daily food. You see, seeking the Kingdom of God implies a striving toward something, not a laissez-faire approach to life.

The Kingdom of God, Basileia tou Teou, in Greek, is prevalent in the New Testament. It is mentioned in almost every parable in the synoptic Gospels, Matthew, Mark, and Luke. While there is no perfect translation of Basileia, many English versions of the Bible translate it as Kingdom, or reign. The Inclusive version has cleverly translated it as kindom, seeking to overcome the image of a masculine monarchy conjured by the word kingdom. Feminist theologians follow the Inclusive Bible's translation. Another critique of the translation of Basileia into kin-dom comes from Ada Maria Isasi-Diaz who first coined the term and argued that *basileia* is not a concept that refers to a territory but to a state of relationships, a moving and changing set of interconnected relationships practiced and lived in justice, equity, and peace.

For today's purpose, I would translate Basileia as home, uplifting the term, kinship, kin-dom, a movement of relationships that constitute our emotional and spiritual home, which is not limited to but includes a geographical and physical sense.

It was Saturday, October 25, 2008, in the afternoon, when I landed at the Saskatoon airport. It was my first time in Saskatoon. Everything was different from my home, Inchon in Korea, or even my first Canadian home in Toronto. The sites and the smells were different. The size of the city was different. Nothing was familiar. To be honest, I felt uneasy. Of course, I was nervous about the job interview at St. Andrew's College. It was for this reason I was in Saskatoon. But it was not just the pressure of the interview. Everything was strange. Would I ever feel at home here, I wondered? On Sunday I spent some time exploring. I visited a church. Actually, the college had assigned a guide for my visit and she drove me around the city and even showed me some houses that were on sale. She said, "don't worry. You will get this job so you need to check some houses." She helped me get the lay of the land. Bless her, I am ever so thankful for her hospitality and her confidence in me.

Despite that, I had a restless Sunday night. When I woke up the next morning, however, the light of the sun did not seem so strange. In fact, it seemed familiar, and seemed to carry a message: "Do not worry. Everything will be all right." With this feeling in my heart, I tried to be brave as I made my way to St. Andrew's College for my interview. On my way I crossed the University Bridge, looking down the river that was swiftly moving below me. When I got to the college, I entered the chapel to pray and suddenly the fear in my heart totally subsided. At that moment, I felt drawn to the center, the communion table. Oval in shape, it stood in the center of the space, surrounded by the pews, which faced in from all directions. Somehow I felt mysteriously welcomed. I felt at home.

From the day I started work at St. Andrew's, I have touched this communion table many times. Besides my own desk at the office, it is the surface upon which I have most often placed things, my hands, a Bible, the communion elements, and my sermon notes. It even beats the tables in the classrooms for the amount I have used it. Bread for the journey, juice for justice, and food for fellowship were shared around that table so many times in countless different ways. You may say I am attached to this oval-shaped communion table of this chapel space. You may say that my body remembers it. It will always have a special place in my heart. Sara Ahmed in *The Cultural Politics of Emotion* says, "Bodies take the shape of the very contact they have with objects and others." Here bodies imply more than physical and biological individual identities. They include religious, social bodies of communities. In this sense, I can say with confidence that I have been shaped emotionally and physically by this object in this space.

Many happy years later, I left Saskatoon and moved back to Toronto. In a way, the move back to Toronto was a risk. Saskatoon had been a strange place but I had made it a home. (Or maybe it had made a home for me.) Leaving meant, leaving home again and searching once more for a home, a new home in what is an old home.

As some of you know from your own experience, migration, leaving a familiar place to an unfamiliar place is never easy. It is painful to make new friends for people like me, who are introverts. It is difficult to learn, unlearn, and relearn to integrate into a new work environment. But migration, a journey of leaving home to find home, is necessary for people of faith. Jesus exhorted us to seek. "Seek first," he said, "the Basileia tou Teou." But what if we are feeling comfortable right where we are? "Seek!," said Jesus. We know that no matter how comfortable and happy we may feel in a place, God calls us to keep striving and seeking a basileia, home, kin-dom, a network of relationships for the sake of eternal life.

There are tons of stories in the Bible that feature people who left home, starting from Adam, Eve, Abraham, Sarah, Hagar, and Moses in Hebrew Bible. In the Christian Scriptures, Jesus, the disciples, the Apostle Paul, and many who he called literally left their homes to follow him. John, the author of the Revelation, the last book of the New Testament, was also of course exiled to the island of Patmos, far from his original home.

In this case, the biblical story of Naomi is somewhat unique, and I find it inspiring. You know the story well. Naomi lived in Bethlehem. Do you know what Bethlehem means? (pause) In Hebrew, it means the house of bread. In Arabic, it means the house of meat. In short, Bethlehem is literally the house of sustenance. One day a famine hit the land of Bethlehem. The house of food became the house of no food. What a paradox! As a people of faith, striving for home, Naomi and her family left home to find home, which was in the land of Moab for them. They lived there for about ten years. Through these years, Naomi would have had joys such as the marriages of her two sons and the growing families with two daughters-in-law. But eventually she also had to face hardships, the loss of these sons and her husband.

Ten years living in one place is a long time, long enough to feel joy and sorrow, long enough to make a home. The land of Moab may have actually been a comfortable place for Naomi after ten years of living there. And in her tragedy, she may well have had friends and extended family around to support her. So why did Naomi decide to leave? Returning to Bethlehem as a widow and with no children was risky. It would not have been a triumphal return. There was little if anything to celebrate and perhaps few to welcome her, especially if they perceived her as a potential burden. While she had heard that her hometown Bethlehem had recovered from the famine, there may have been no guarantee that this home would once again become the house of bread for her. There would have been no guarantee that she would have no worries about what to eat. In fact, she would have known that she would likely be a target for gossip and contempt. We don't know why she left home to return to her old home, which was no longer home. But we know that such things often happen to God's people.

"Seek first the kin-dom of God!" This was Jesus's exhortation. In our coming and our going, in good times and in bad, the kin-dom is over the horizon. Seek it! Seek it and do not worry. Blessings come on the road. We will be clothed with beauty even as those lilies we pass by are clothed. We will be fed, even as the birds that fly above us are fed. Do not worry for yourself. But seek the well-being of others you meet, seek to feed the hunger, seek to provide the thirsty with a cup of water, and so forth. In so doing, we shall seek peace and shout with joy. That is the promise and the Basileia tou Teou.

NOTES

1. Don M. Wardlaw, ed., *Learning Preaching: Understanding and Participating in the Process* (Lincoln: Lincoln College and Seminary Press and the Academy of Homiletics, 1989).

2. Thomas G. Long and Leonora Tubbs Tisdale, eds., *Teaching Preaching as a Christian Practice: A New Approach to Homiletical Pedagogy* (Louisville: Westminster/John Knox, 2008), 12.

3. Craig Dykstra and Dorothy Bass, "A Theological Understanding of Christian Practices," in *Practicing Theology: Beliefs and Practices in Christian Life*, ed. Miroslav Volf and Dorothy Bass (Grand Rapids: Eerdmans, 2002), 18.

4. Maria Harris, *Fashion Me a People: Curriculum in the Church* (Louisville: Westminster/John Knox, 1989).

5. World Council of Churches, *Baptism, Eucharist, and Ministry* (Geneva: WCC, 1982). Dirk G. Lange and Dwight W. Vogel, eds., *Ordo: Bath, Word, Prayer, Table: A Liturgical Primer in Honor of Gordon W. Lathrop* (Akron: OSL, 2005).

6. *Celebrate God's Presence: A Book of Services for The United Church of Canada* (Toronto: United Church Publishing House, 2000).

7. Anna Carter Florence, *Rehearsing Scripture: Discovering God's Word in Community* (Grand Rapids: Eerdmans, 2018), viii.

8. John McClure, *The Roundtable Pulpit: Where Leadership and Preaching Meet* (Nashville: Abingdon, 1995), 59.

9. Florence, *Rehearsing Scripture*, 165–203. These five are gathering, numbering, encountering, speaking, and sharing that examine verbs, nouns, adjectives, and ratios.

10. John E. Burkhart, *Worship: A Searching Examination of the Liturgical Experience* (Philadelphia: Westminster Press, 1982), 31–32.

11. Don E. Saliers, *Worship as Theology: Foretastes of Glory Divine* (Nashville: Abingdon 1994), 176.

12. Craigo-Snell, *The Empty Church*, 88.

13. Florence, *Preaching as Testimony*, 90. Ron Allen uses this term throughout *Interpreting the Gospel: An Introduction to Preaching* (St. Louis: Chalice, 1998).

14. Ruth Duck, *Worship for the Whole People of God: Vital Worship for the 21st Century* (Louisville: Westminster John Knox, 2013), 15.

15. Kim-Cragg, *Interdependence*, 68.

16. The Murphy Center for Liturgical Research, *Made, Not Born: New Perspectives on Christian Initiation and the Catechumenate* (Notre Dame: University of Notre Dame Press, 1976).

17. Tom Long, *The Witness of Preaching* (Louisville: Westminster/John Knox, 2005), 173.

18. Charles Bartow, *The Preaching Moment* (Nashville: Abingdon, 1980).

19. Ashcroft, and et al., *The Empire Writes Back*, 36–37.

20. Loretta Dorniseh, "Symbolic Systems and the Interpretation of Scripture: An Introduction to the Work of Paul Ricoeur," *Semeia* 4 (1975): 1–26.

21. Paul Ricoeur, *Time and Narrative*, volume 1, trans. Kathleen McLaughlin and David Pellauer (Chicago: University of Chicago Press, 1984), 5–30.

22. Allen, *Patterns of Preaching: A Sermon Sampler* (St. Louis: Chalice, 1998), 98–103.

23. Sarah J. Smith, *Hearing Sermon: Reader-Response Theory as a Basis for a Listener-Response Homiletic* (PhD Dissertation, Emmanuel College, University of Toronto, 2002).

24. HyeRan Kim-Cragg, S*tory and Song: A Postcolonial Interplay between Christian Education and Worship* (New York: Peter Lang, 2012), 30.

25. https://www.ndtv.com/world-news/donald-trump-to-congresswomen-go-back-where-you-came-from-2069521

26. Miroslave Volf, "Theology for a Way of Life," in *Practicing Theology: Beliefs and Practices in Christian Life*, ed. Miroslav Volf and Dorothy Bass (Grand Rapids: Eerdmans, 2002), 250–254.

27. David N. Power, "The Holy Spirit: Scripture, Tradition, and Interpretation," in *Keeping the Faith: Essays to Mark the Centenary of Lux Mundi*, ed. Geoffrey Wainwright (Philadelphia: Fortress, 1988), 169.

28. Walter Brueggemann, *Finally Comes the Poet* (Minneapolis: Fortress, 1989), 7.

29. Alexander Schumemann, *The Eucharist: Sacrament of the Kingdom* (Crestwood, N. Y.: St. Vladimir's Seminary Press, 1988).

30. Yves Congar, "Sacramental Worship and Preaching," in *The Renewal of Preaching: Theory and Practice, Vol. 33 of Concilium*, ed. Karl Rahner, trans. Theodore L. Westow (New York: Paulist, 1968), 62.

31. Claudio Carvalhaes, "Storytelling Renewed," in *The Renewed Homiletic*, ed. O. Wesley Allen Jr. (Minneapolis: Fortress, 2010), 35–39.

32. Jennifer Lord, "Sacraments, Preaching and Teaching Of," in *New Interpreter's Handbook of Preaching*, ed. Paul Scott Wilson (Nashville: Abingdon, 2008), 284.

33. Stephen Moore and Mayra Rivera, eds., *Planetary Loves: Spivak, Postcoloniality, and Theology* (New York: Fordham University Press, 2011).

34. Burton Z. Cooper and John S. McClure, *Claiming Theology in the Pulpit* (Louisville: Westminster John Knox, 2003), 129.

Chapter 2

Imagination

Proclaiming a New World beyond Our Immediate Grasp

God has scattered the proud in the thoughts of their hearts. God has brought down the powerful from their thrones, and lifted up the lowly. God has filled the hungry with good things, and sent the rich away empty.

—Luke 1:51–53

The nature of the ripple effect is that each wave influences the next waves, reinforcing one another. The metaphor of postcolonial preaching as creating a ripple effect points to the connectivity of its different aspects: the first circle of rehearsal is connected to the next circle that is imagination. The rehearsal of the realm of God is inseparably connected to a capacity to imagine that realm, the here-and-now-but-not-yet reality. A new and renewed world, the kin-dom of God that is breaking into the present reality, relies on the capacity to imagine. Postcolonial preaching is "the voice of the imagination."[1] To develop such a voice is to learn to write a sermon with our ears. It is to hear the message with our eyes, as a Buddhist wisdom exhorts the people to "see the sounds of pain."[2] Imagination as anticipation is the greatest source of human delight, filled with surprises. The preaching imagination combined with the practice of rehearsal enables people to dream a different world, living out a reality that is not readily obvious and barely audible. It is rehearsing that reality daily. It is living as if the world has not succumbed to the powers and principalities. Preaching provides a capacity to see beyond the status quo and is attuned to voices that are muted, metaphorically speaking. Preaching imagination is about dreaming the impossible. It is about greeting the future that has yet to come. In this regard, the preaching imagination may most fit with the liturgical season of Advent. The news that Mary was pregnant with the baby Jesus, the future Messiah, takes an imaginative leap in the face of a brutal reality. While this news was unexpected, Mary would no doubt have been dreaming a new world. She, therefore, had been rehearsing a different world. That is why this news of her unplanned pregnancy had not crushed this young unmarried girl. She had a power within her imagination to face this challenge and any negative reactions she may encounter.

Imagination is beyond words. Mary could hear music in the air as her ancestors whispered in her ears. Mary sang of the radical reordering of the world as she remembered what God has done in the past: God has scattered the proud in the thoughts of their hearts; brought down the powerful from their thrones, and lifted up the lowly, filled the hungry with good things; and sent the rich away empty (Luke 1: 51b–53). Inspired by the faithful response of Mary, a postcolonial preaching imagination strives for the proper tension and balance that must exist between the gravity of the world and its problems and the transcendent hope, which it leaps into a world that is yet to be.

Christine Smith named imagination as one of the most important elements in preaching. For her, it is not an artistic luxury but a vital necessity in homiletics.[3] Similarly Kathleen Fischer writes, "[the] imagination not only shows us a possible future" but also evokes the energies needed today "to participate in the coming of that future."[4] Imagination is both about the future and about today as the rehearsal of the realm of God is also about an awaited future and today's practice. Uplifting the work of Gerald Green, who defines imagination as an ability "to see what something is like based on one's prior experience,"[5] Eunjoo Mary Kim notes that imagining a new reality as a lived reality is possible because it is rooted in people's prior knowledge or previous experiences.[6] Here I note how connected memory of the past is to an imagined future. Taking from these scholars' contributions, I also stress how central prior and present experiences are for building up the preaching imagination. To receive that gift of imagination, the preacher sometimes needs to take an arduous journey, what Fred Craddock called, "the longest trip."[7] Craddock imagined this as a journey between the head and the heart, between abstract thought and lived experience.

The capacity to imagine is crucial in postcolonial preaching. The postcolonial world is marked by a series of experiences filled with injustices and inequalities particular to this moment that must be overcome. It requires imagination to understand the ways that our neighbor may be affected by lingering colonial and neocolonial forces that continue to drag people down and crush them underfoot. Racism, displacement, homelessness, and poverty are all part of the postcolonial world. But so is the possibility of overcoming these realities, signified by the "post" in postcolonial. Those who have engaged in postcolonial scholarship know that no one is claiming that the impact of colonialism has been completely overcome. The "post" in postcolonialism does not signify this. Instead, it recognizes that while we have already moved out of a colonial stage of history, many of the patterns of colonization remain intact. Postcolonialism has that already but not yet sensibility built into its thinking. Furthermore, postcolonial theorists declare that a new, just, and reconciled reality is manifesting itself through billions of people seeking to shed this ugly past. The "beyond" is an important aspect of postcolonial thought in this regard, connecting the past and the future.[8] Postcolonial thinkers want to move beyond present realities into something that has yet to be fully grasped.[9] Such is the challenge of the imagination.

In this chapter, once we establish the necessity of imagination in preaching, we will make a connection between imagination and the realm of God, followed by the deep connection between imagination and language and imagination and scripture. We will continue to examine the preaching imagination scripture in relation to the paradox captured in scripture. Finally, we will explore the postcolonial imagination as historical, dialogical, and diasporic as suggested by Kwok Pui-lan and draw homiletical implications by presenting a sermon as an example.

IMAGINATION AND THE REHEARSAL OF THE KIN-DOM OF GOD

Preaching imagination is a skill, a disciplined practice that needs to be learned and improved by training.[10] Anna Carter Florence emphasizes the need to practice imagination:

> There are many preachers and teachers of preaching who assume imagination has to do with learning fancy new methods or techniques or adding some ingredient.... In my view, nothing could be farther from the truth, or worse for preaching. Imagination is not an ingredient you add. It is a muscle you develop, and it doesn't happen overnight.... You have to work at it, exercise it, to get in the habit of using it, living by it, seeing through it, every day.... [Imagination] *does* take sweat and discipline and a commitment to routine.[11]

Here we see a close connection between rehearsal and imagination for achieving excellence in preaching. Both require the work of homiletical discipline. Rehearsing and practicing imagination demand an intentional and regular effort. Preaching is a necessary constant of the Christian condition. If we are Christian, we preach. The ways Christians have preached over the millennia has changed but the Good News has not. This is what we mean by the constancy of preaching. The constancy of preaching presumes that we are always compelled to do it.

The preaching imagination is not a solitary practice. It is absurd to think that a preacher could preach in isolation from others. The realm of God cannot be imagined as a monologue, so to speak. It needs multiple actors and spectators. How could one create a world (kin-dom) without one's kin, the community?! It is a question and an exclamation. People need to imagine a new world together. The church, ecclesia, as a gathered community is an immediate (albeit not the only) context of preaching. The work of homiletical imagination is intertwined with the imagination of the community. It largely depends on the wisdom dwelling in the community rather than a special gift or ability of the preacher. Tom Troeger likens ones' imagination to a grafted tree branch. He writes, you "graft your creativity to the richly rooted, thickly branched tree that has been cultivated by the entire community, that tree that is its heritage, its tradition of song and prayer, praise and proclamation, survival and resistance."[12] In addition to the significance of the community involved in the work of imagination, the well-being of the community is bound up with this same imagination, a vision of justice. This vision born of the preaching imagination is like lifeblood pumping through the veins of those who are suffering systematic oppression and historical injustice. Such is the effect of the *Magnificat* in Luke 1. The Song of Mary echoes through the ages, singing of dignity and freedom, calling for an end to power that oppresses the weak and the vulnerable.

IMAGINATION AND LANGUAGE

Language can serve as a spark for the imagination. Often it is the tension between two words or two meanings within a word that sparks a third meaning, which is different from and beyond either.[13] The ideograms of East Asian script provide many examples of new meanings that springs from the combination of opposites. Furthermore, meaning-making through the creation of additional words in language funds the imagination in preaching. For example, "rest," 休 in Chinese is a combination of two words, human (人) and tree (木). The notion of resting, therefore, is conjured up by an image of a person beside a tree. Only the imagination sees the deep relationship between humans and trees and the way the one produces a restful environment for the other. This is an understanding that was not far from the Hebrew imagination in scripture. The image in Psalm 1 of one who meditates on the Torah and becomes "like trees planted by streams of water" (Ps. 1:3) evokes the notion of sabbath restfulness. Here biblical and East Asian imagination strengthen and deepen one another.

The East Asian character for "home" is another example. This character combines two unrelated ideograms, 宀, meaning roof and 豕, meaning pig. This character is pronounced "ka" in Korean and written as "家." The idea is that if we have a roof and an animal together, then we have a home for a human. This juxtaposition may not seem obvious to us these days. While it is easy to understand how a roof could be associated with home because of the protection it provides, we may wonder why the word pig is needed. The reason may not be too far from those of us with farming experiences. In fact, living with animals was not so uncommon in Western societies not so long ago and remains a reality for many in the world still today. In the case of China, and many parts of Asia, pigs were great companions of human families because their presence (and odor) discouraged other bothersome creatures, such as poisonous snakes and insects, from approaching and harming humans. But this insight shares a deep connection with the Gospel story as well as it harkens back to our Christmas story of Jesus being born in a barn. This idea of home further communicates the important notion of a symbiotic relationship between humans and animals. It shows how interdependent and interconnected we are.

The postcolonial preacher would do well to tap into linguistic wisdom embedded in languages other than English and cultures other than those that are dominant in their community. Other languages and cultures will only expand the imagination of postcolonial preaching. The work of seeking to understand different cultures and languages is critical in a world where cultural and linguistic diversity is under threat. This task becomes homiletically and theologically urgent as our imagination of the possibilities of God's existence and nature are reduced by the narrowest interpretations or overused metaphors. When that happens, preaching becomes inaccessible to the preacher and the congregation. Diverse cultural and linguistic wisdom not only promises to increase our capacity to relate to our neighbor but can also lead to a deeper appreciation of the interconnectedness of all life. Pondering the imaginative energy contained in words will provide tools to overcome anthropocentric worldviews and imagine a world where ecological justice flows like a mighty river.

IMAGINATION AND SCRIPTURE

The preaching imagination needs constantly to grow and improve. To cultivate the imagination, one must find sources to nurture it. Scripture offers supple inspiration for enhancing the imagination. The realm of God is best revealed in scripture where life-giving relationships and lessons for shared living can be found. Take, for example, the prophecy of Jeremiah: "I am the Lord; I act with steadfast love, justice, and righteousness in the earth for in these things I delight, says the LORD" (Jer. 9:23–24). The response to this divine fidelity is found in a rediscovery of the relational nature of human and ecological life where the care of others, the dignity of self, and the trust in God are nurtured.[14] When humans adequately respond to God's fidelity, joy comes even to the barren wastelands of the earth (Isa. 35:1). Through the poetic imagination of the Bible, humans can see and hear mountain and fields clapping their hands and find themselves living in a creation that is deeply interconnected (Isa. 55:12).

The scriptural proclamation of the creation praising God imagines a radical, faithful, daring new world. The message spoken through the mouths of prophets, as Walter Brueggemann writes, cannot be understood without appreciating "poetic ambiguity, elusive playfulness, always being underway and in negotiation, ready always to be surprised."[15] To imagine is to contradict the taken-for-granted world around us. Preaching from imagination, scripturally speaking, is to become an "epistemological misfit"[16] in the eyes of the world. To engage in imagination is therefore to find oneself in the tradition of social misfits through the ages who have manifested their nonconformity through such actions as civil disobedience.[17]

The preaching imagination needs to be "uttered" (as in proclaimed) to construe a world other than the one in which we currently live. This utterance is theological because God is imagined not as an *irrelevant transcendence* a *cozy immanence* but as "a real character" and "an effective agent"[18] in our world. God is the main character of wonder and the chief agent of nourishment in the feast of imagination for postcolonial preaching. We can witness this kind of preaching revealed in the books of the prophets where God used the lips of these poetic utterers to cultivate imagination of the hearers toward the inbreaking of justice, peace, and love.

The postcolonial interpretation of the scripture is particularly helpful for the preaching imagination. R. S. Sugirtharajah contends that the imagination is absolutely essential in a postcolonial world where "the future is open and the past unstable and constantly changing."[19] Kwok Pui-lan calls for a need to engage postcolonial criticism when interpreting the Bible: "The Bible lends itself to postcolonial and intercultural studies because it deals with the themes of travel, space and spatial construction, movement, boundaries, borderland, border-crossing, crossroads, indigenized women and populations, ethnic formation, diasporic communities, rhizomic fragments, uprooting, displacing place, displacement, transplantation, international power relations, and globalization processes."[20] Postcolonial critique aims to expose the colonial history, and its legacies so that the present reality does not repeat the past mistakes but is informed by the critique in a way that corrects the present and constructs a more just and viable future.

IMAGINATION AND PARADOX

To engage in postcolonial preaching is to hold contradictions in a creative tension and embrace paradox. To proclaim the good news that the last shall be the first (Mark 10:31) is paradoxical and imaginative. Christ's lesson that in order to gain eternal life, we must learn to lose it (Matt. 10:39) is one that takes imagination. The preaching imagination embraces the paradox that emptying oneself for the sake of Christ one becomes full in Christ (Phil. 2:8).

The preaching imagination embraces reversals of fortune. Mary Donovan Turner captures this paradoxical insight as she explores the preaching of Miriam in Exodus.[21] Miriam sings of how the God of the weak has triumphed gloriously and the throne of the powerful has been thrown into the sea (Exod. 15:20–21). Miriam's song is picked up by the song of Hannah who praised the divine paradox: the bows of the mighty are broken, but the feeble gird on strength. Those who were full go empty and those who were hungry are filled. God will make the rich poor and the poor rich. God brings the high low and exalts the lowly (1 Sam. 2:1–10). Finally, Mary the mother of Jesus takes up the tune proclaiming that God is "casting down the proud and the exalting the lowly" (Luke 1).

Mary's song is a prime example of the preaching paradox. In her imagination of a new world, the paradox of God, the paradox of faith, and the paradox of life are proclaimed. In the *Magnificat*, Mary expresses a deep gratitude to God who lifted up someone like her and exalts her son who would be born in a manger, the lowest of places. The paradox of Christianity culminates in the proclamation that the one who is crucified is the Messiah, that the Word is also the Flesh. The extravagant and unpredictable reign of God becomes the paradox that runs through and across the whole narrative of scripture.[22]

The preaching imagination opens the eyes of the community to that, which is otherwise impossible to see. Mary Elizabeth Moore writes, "God is more than meets the eye—present and visible, yet mysterious and invisible; part of daily life, yet pulling life toward eschatological hope; caring for the smallest and humblest parts of creation, yet seeing in them more than others see."[23] Florence makes a similar claim: to preach imagination is "to believe in something that is invisible." It is to be sure of "a promise that has yet to be fulfilled." Preaching imagination is to "keep hoping, beyond reason and well past the expiration date."[24] To preach is to imagine the world that is coming as if we were already living in it. The preaching imagination is a contradiction, that is truth, a source of hope and a matter of trust. Through the preaching imagination, people can almost grasp that untouchable, unseen, and inaudible reality. This is beautifully expressed in the homily to the Hebrews: "faith is the assurance of things hoped for, the conviction of things not seen" (Heb. 11:1).

The wisdom from the ancestors in faith captured in this homily reminds us that the preaching imagination is not only work for the future but also the work of remembering the past. We can recall the memories of history as the work of imagination. Retelling the story of the past with imagination as an active remembrance harnesses the possibility of reconstructing the history of those who have been dismissed as insignificant. The story of captivity retold and remembered in preaching releases imagination and brings freedom. The story of dictatorship retold and remembered calls forth democracy.

The preaching imagination reveals the absurdity of injustice. It has a way of turning our world upside down, just as the songs of Miriam, Hannah, and Mary do. It is the key to see how God surrendered to the power in order to defeat it, and died on a Roman cross in order to rise victoriously into a world free of colonizers. This paradoxical faith is rippling out as a reality as we participate in the protest for Black Lives Matter and the plight of migrants, especially undocumented workers from many parts of the world. This current reality unearths the historical fact that the white Americas (United States and Canada) were built on indigenous land, and with the backbreaking work of African slaves and Asian laborers. Exposing this history is paradoxical because the wealth was accumulated at the price of their lives yet, these lives who contributed to astronomical wealth have been treated as if they are worth nothing, as if their lives do not matter. Postcolonial theorist Gayatri Spivak proclaims, "as the North continues ostensibly to 'aid' the South—as formerly imperialism 'civilized' the New World—the South's crucial assistance to the North in keeping up its resource-hungry style is forever foreclosed."[25] To disclose the foreclosed violence and dependency as a task of postcolonial preaching, one needs to further explore aspects of postcolonial imagination, a task to which we now turn.

THE HISTORICAL, DIALOGICAL, AND DIASPORIC TRAJECTORIES OF THE PREACHING IMAGINATION

From a postcolonial perspective, imagination is one of the most critical capacities to have in preaching. Kwok Pui-lan writes, "to imagine means to discern that something is not fitting, to search for new images, and to arrive at new patterns of meaning and interpretation. . . . For what we cannot imagine, we cannot live into and struggle for."[26] As a theologizing and theorizing principle, she offers historical, dialogical, and diasporic trajectories as three critical movements of postcolonial imagination for doing theology. Her offering is instructive in contouring postcolonial preaching. Kwok's standing among Christian postcolonial thinkers is widely recognized and her ideas provide important material for building up a concept of what the preaching imagination needs to do in our postcolonial world.

Historical Imagination

History in the postcolonial imagination does not merely refer to a record from the past but points to a perspectival discourse for the sake of creating a living memory for the present and the future. Elizabeth Schüssler Fiorenza's feminist theological insights share much in common with Kwok's regarding history as she works to reconstruct the memory of women and others who struggle to find a place in the present-day ecclesiology of the Roman Catholic Church.[27] The reconstruction of the past requires imagination because it is difficult, if not impossible, to thoroughly detect the past realities of oppressed, illiterate, and marginalized groups. In many cases, these groups were unable to leave an historical record of their own experiences and perspectives. Imagination with a sense of wonder is necessary to weave fragmented pieces of history into a more complete whole.

Historical imagination is provisional. Florence provides wise advice in this regard: "what looks like a faithful imagination in one time and context may look quite different with the passage of time [in different contexts].... We can only interpret the best we can, helping and leaving room for the Spirit to make itself heard in the voice of the community as well as in the questions—and new musical rhythms—of outsiders."[28] The histories we are able to tell with the help of imagination, therefore, are only as useful as they are responsive to the present context. The acknowledgment of the provisional nature of history engenders humility. Postcolonial preaching, therefore, needs to be humble and learn from less dominant and more marginalized historical perspectives. Commitment to this learning means a commitment to developing a postcolonial imagination.

Learning history using the postcolonial imagination also means working to liberate people from an old and enslaving history. This is a critical task of postcolonial preaching when the history is distorted and tainted by a dominant and dominating narrative. That is what Kwok means when she writes, "The historical imagination aims . . . to release the past so that the present is livable."[29] The preaching imagination with a postcolonial historical trajectory is about ushering in a future of new and life-giving possibility. Venturing into this hopeful future requires poetic utterance and daring metaphors. But it also needs to be grounded in historical imagination. In short, our future needs to be connected to the past.

Dialogical Imagination

Dialogical imagination is mainly concerned with the person who is doing the imagining. In the postcolonial context, where a plurality of voices speaking different social dialects from all sorts of backgrounds are coming together in new and urgent ways, dialogical imagination is an essential tool to allow those voices to converse with one another and speak constructively together. But even more complex than a cacophony of voices speaking at the same time, the dialogical imagination is also tasked with hearing that merges across times. These voices travel through time as repeated utterances, written, interpreted, and commented upon. Kwok explains that dialogical imagination involves a polyvocal speech, which is

> of speech within speech, utterance within utterance, and at the same time also speech about speech, utterance about utterance. We have to understand the dynamic interrelationship between the speech being reported and the speech doing the reporting. This requires us to pay attention to the relation between oral transmission and the written document of the Bible, the framing of discourse by the author, the multilevels of the dialogue, and the possibilities of reframing the retelling in the present situation.[30]

Dialogical imagination helps us to expose the many layers of voices in a text and how certain voices may be privileged at the expense of others to the detriment of justice and right relations.

Postcolonial biblical scholar Benny Liew, drawing from his cultural and ancestral Chinese wisdom, suggests the idea of having "yin and yang eyes"[31] in reading the biblical text. This bifocal vision is an ability to see the living and the dead, hearing the voices who passed away and hearing the voices who are alive. Yin and yang eyes are indispensable for understanding the story of the family of Jesus as they fled into Egypt in the Gospel of Matthew. Yin and yang eyes can interpret the story through the lens of East Asian culture to see the significance of the threat faced by the ancestors of this family whose two-year-old eldest male baby was in danger of being slaughtered. At the same time, they behold a hopeful future becoming reality through the resistance of the family of Jesus as they escape the violence (the present tense of the Gospel).

Dialogical imagination helps preachers interpret the texts containing the words of the dead while maintaining a conversation with the context of the living. However, dialogue is not an equal process. Not every voice is at the table and even if they are, they are often misrepresented or tokenized. The role of dialogical imagination is essential in this asymmetrical reality because it exposes how often any interaction with different cultures and traditions is imbued with power and authority. It is that unequal power created through a lengthy and complicated colonial process that we need to acknowledge to leverage and dismantle through the power of imagination.

Diasporic Imagination

Diasporic imagination is born of the postcolonial process of navigating different cultures and traditions in a context of increasing global migration. The emergence of diaspora communities has become one of the most notable global phenomena in the twenty-first century. This is a legacy of colonialism and involves in large measure the forced displacement of millions upon millions of people. The late postcolonial scholar Stuart Hall has said, "The 'post-colonial' world is always-already 'diasporic.'"[32] This is also why migration has become a theological locus of the twenty-first century.[33] The prevalence of migration raises questions about the meaning of home, belonging, and borders. It gives rise to ideas about fluid identity and cultural hybridity. In the Christian preaching tradition, the diasporic nature of our spiritual reality is often affirmed in a positive sense, and connected to the experiences of foremothers and fathers for whom their displacement and journey to find a new home was part of their experience of God. Our God is a God on the move, so to speak. Being Christian, in this regard, is to have the diasporic identity of one who God calls to leave home to find home. However, migration is never easy. Indeed, it is often painful, especially when it is forced and involuntary. Thus, diasporic imagination helps us to recognize the scar of the migration experience. It marks the trauma of the loss of home, memory, language, culture, and even loved ones, while carving out a journey toward healing.[34]

Diasporic imagination is captured in the historical trajectory of the Exodus in biblical traditions. Diasporic imagination is also uttered in the biblical narratives of new rebirth in the depth of exile. The prophet Isaiah as the poet, recalling the story of Genesis with historical imagination, reached all the way back to Sarah for new possibilities.[35] Isaiah connects the very first foremother of faith with a vision for future generations.

> Sing, O barren one who did not bear; burst into song and shout, you who have not been in labor! For the children of the desolate woman will be more than the children of her that is married, says the LORD. Enlarge the site of your tent, and let the curtains of your habitations be stretched out; do not hold back; lengthen your cords and strengthen your stacks. For you will spread out to the right and to the left, and your descendants will possess the nations and will settle the desolate towns (Isa. 54:1–3).

In summary, Kwok's three movements of postcolonial imagination—historical, dialogical, and diasporic—unearth some of the content essential to the preaching imagination in a postcolonial context. This content addresses realities related to historical oppression, dialogical diversity, and migration. The historical imagination probes "behind" scripture, while the dialogical imagination navigates in "between" of the multiple voices of interpretation. Finally, the diasporic imagination looks to see "before" the text the current reality of migration that is shaping the future of our communities of faith.

The following sermon features a reflection on Joseph and his experience of the Christmas event. Centering Joseph requires imagination, a leap from the typical Christmas story, which is usually centered around the baby Jesus and the mother Mary. The sermon also incorporates Kwok's historical, dialogical, and diasporic trajectories of postcolonial imagination as the narrator invites the congregation to imagine the life of Joseph's family as refugees. Also, the preacher identifies her family's war experience as an historical trajectory of postcolonial reality connecting with the present reality of the congregation and the story of the Bible. The sermon can be imagined as a play, involving multiple voices: Joseph, angel, narrator, and preacher.

SERMON EXAMPLE

"Piercing Stars and Daring Visits"

Matt. 2: 13–23

Preacher's voice:

My family has had many Christmas visitors over the past number of years. Since my spouse has been serving a congregation, it has been impossible for us to visit somewhere else at Christmas. As a result, my family has always hosted the visits rather than been hosted. While it is a wonderful gift to be able to host loved ones in our own home, there is something very nice about being a guest too.

Hosting and visiting are a big part of the Christmas story. This year, as I read over the Christmas story, I thought about Joseph, how we were visited and how he hosted his visitors. As I read and thought about him, I began to hear his voice in a way I hadn't heard before. I would like to invite you to hear that voice today. So shall we visit Joseph?

Narrator's Voice:

It all starts in chapter 1 of the Gospel of Matthew. Joseph was visited by an angel. It was a dream visit and an unexpected visit. This is lucky for Joseph because it meant he didn't have to clean the house or do any cooking to get ready. In that respect, he got off easy. But on the other hand, you couldn't say that it was an easy visit! Joseph was getting ready for his wedding with Mary, when the angelic visitor broke the shocking news that his finance would be having a baby who wasn't his! Talk about a life-changing visit.

Joseph's Voice:

"No way," Joseph thought, "the marriage is over. I'm going to have to divorce Mary" (though he would do so without shaming her because that would be deadly to her and he wasn't that kind of person).

Narrator's Voice:

But then, no sooner had he made up his mind than he realized he could not do that. Joseph could not articulate why exactly in words or in any rational sense. It was hard to swallow the fact that he had to live a life with Mary, without knowing what happened to her. It made no sense. But deep in his heart, he knew he had to do what did not make sense.

The angel had told him that his child would be the Messiah, the most longed for person of the Jewish faith. He could hardly believe that the baby was conceived by the Holy Spirit. His brain was filled with emotions. But it was not the religious message that impacted him the most.

Suddenly, Joseph felt tired. It was all so overwhelming. He could not imagine that he would become a dad. But the baby was coming, whether he was prepared or not. Joseph had to get ready. There were things to prepare, from cleaning to cooking, from packing to wrapping.

(pause to imagine all the activity)
Soon after the baby Jesus was born, Joseph had another unexpected visit.

This time it was people from the far east. The timing wasn't great. Who wants to host important visitors you don't even know, days after you have become a dad for the first time! On top of hosting so many visits from his family and her family seeing a new-born baby and looking after the mother Mary, Joseph had to host these visitors as well. But this visit was special. The Magi, these complete strangers, brought precious gifts to their child. They bowed to the baby Jesus. Joseph heard the story that they followed the star. It was the star that led them to pay a visit to their son Jesus who would save and become the hope for the world.

In the midst of this highly unusual visit, Joseph was still wrestling with the emotions of becoming a father. Already his relationship with Jesus's mom had had some real ups and downs. It was all so confusing, and this new responsibility was not truly awesome. But he was committed to Mary and he knew from his heart that he would look after their baby Jesus.

Joseph's Voice:

"Maybe there is a way," He said to himself, "Mary and I, we will get through this together."

Preacher's Voice:

We all need a good rest after we have hosted many visitors. Hosting takes a lot of work. And I am one of those people who needs a good sleep on an ordinary day. I get really cranky if my sleep is interrupted. Growing up, my family called me a cat because I could cuddle up my small body and find a small corner to sleep whenever I needed a nap.

One day my family was moving. Our house was completely chaotic. The whole place was turned upside down. Movers were in and out. There is no bed, there is no couch, but I needed a nap. As a kid the change was causing me some stress. My sleep had been disturbed the night before. My head was spinning, my eyes were sandy, feeling sore. I was getting cranky. Well, I saw a portable wardrobe, so I went in and cuddled myself up in there. I closed my eyes and fell asleep. Then suddenly I woke up. My bed was moving! The movers were trying to lift the closet to the truck. "Hey," said one of the movers, "Why is this closet so heavy?" They opened the door and found me. I was disappointed to be woken up so early. I'm sure that Jesus got a better sleep in the manger!!! But back to Joseph.

Narrator's Voice:

Joseph must have felt grateful when the Magi visit was over, and everyone had gone home. Joseph was tired. He was overwhelmed. He needed a good rest.

He needed a long uninterrupted sleep. So, he went to bed and fell fast asleep for a second, until:

Angel's Voice:

"Get up, take the child and his mother, and flee to Egypt, and remain there until I tell you; for Herod is about to search for the child to destroy him."

Narrator's Voice:

Oh my goodness! Joseph had just been visited again! Another visit from the angel! But this was even more stressful than the last time. Despite the difficult news in the first visit, the angel's voice had been calming. "Do not be afraid," the angel had whispered. The angel had comforted Joseph saying that he and his family would be all right. More than that, the voice was reassuring, telling him that they would be blessed, and God would be with them through their child, Emmanuel.

This time, however, was different. The voice was urgent; it signaled that there was danger ahead. Joseph, it warned, must not be idle. He must not hesitate.

Joseph's Voice:

"Darn," (Joseph sighed) "so much for a break, so much for a good long sleep."

Narrator's Voice:

He pulled himself up out of bed and faced this new challenge. Joseph checked Mary and the baby beside him; they looked peaceful, blissfully ignorant of the brutality of life. For a moment he was mesmerized, dazed by the beauty of the vision. So peaceful. He could not disturb them. Then, suddenly, the words of the angel came back to him like a pin pricking a bubble. They had to move now. The baby's life depended on it.

Joseph's Voice:

"Wake up!" he shook and said to Mary, "I know you are tired. You have more reason to be than I do. But we have to get up. We must escape. We've got to move." No time to clean-up, no time to cook, minimal time to pack up and leave.

Narrator's Voice:

By this time, they were on the road, Joseph's head was no longer foggy and spinning. His mind was clear, as clear as the winter air. He began to hear the voice of the angel again "Emmanuel God is with us!" He could not put it in words, but he realized that he was not alone and that his family, though in danger, was not alone either.

There was hope. Just as Mary had struggled in the pain and labor of childbirth, so too he must now strain his mind and body and bring life out of this situation.

Then, Joseph remembered the visit of the Magi, what they told him about the star. It was the star that guided them. It was this inextinguishable light, undefeatable shining hope that found them. It was this star, this resilient flickering star that gave the visitors daring courage to risk their lives, to mock Herod the King, and trick him. Joseph finally realized what this visit of the Magi and this warning visit from the angel meant.

Yes, it is true that those gifts they brought were generous. Their deep and reverent bow, the gesture of worshipping the baby Jesus was awesome, too. But for Joseph as he prepared with his family to take a journey into the unknown, it was their journey following the star through the darkness that seemed most important. That daring vision was what Joseph and his family needed just then.

Preacher's Voice:

The journey Joseph took with his family was like the journey that my own parents took to escape the Korean War in 1951. It was 4th of January. It was bitterly cold. It was pitch black at night. They walked on the frozen Daedong river of North Korea that ran across the heavy guarded border into South Korea. It was a dangerous journey. But they had to risk their lives and pack up their belongings and leave their home to save their life.

Joseph's journey was also like the journey that the refugee families that we heard about on the news took when they left their home and settled in our city. It is like the journey that the refugees our church sponsored took when they fled the violence against transgendered people in their country to arrive here with the help of our congregation a month ago.

Narrator's Voice:

Joseph is still not 100 percent sure what happened to Mary and her pregnancy. He is still not so sure about Jesus becoming the Messiah. But he is very sure that the time has come for his family to strike out into the unknown. He does not know what that journey will look like and how much more danger will visit him and confront his family.

One thing was for sure, however, for Joseph amid this uncertainty, this perilous and painstaking migration journey. He knew that the light of the stars would guide him through the night. The star of hope, peace, joy, and love.

Preacher's Voice:

There. That is a nice way to end the story, don't you think? As we listened to the Christmas story this year, as we reflected on the story of Joseph and the many remarkable visitors he entertained, we give thanks for him and his family. We give thanks to God, Emmanuel.

This Christmas let us remember that we are the light of Christ. I do not have trouble remembering this because the light of the loving hearts of this church like the stars that led the Magi has blessed me over years and continues to guide and watch over me. Let us continue to love one another. Let us shine our light outside these walls, too. There are many that need the guidance of love in their lives.

As we wrap up our Christmas time, put away our Christmas things and get ready to greet the new year, I pray that we all take time to marvel at the journey, to catch a Holy moment and look upon the stars. I hope that you are visited by the wonder of the stars, and like Mary and Joseph will treasure the memories of the other visits you have had. And if we are ever forced to rise to a dangerous challenge, may the comforting words of the angel, "Do not be afraid, God is with you," ring in our ears and light our path for a long, long time.

NOTES

1. Lawrence Thompson and R. H. Winnick, *Robert Frost* (New York: Holt, Rinehart & Winston, 1981), 172.
2. Kim-Cragg, *Interdependence*, 55, 144.
3. Christine Smith, *Weaving the Sermon: Preaching in a Feminist Perspective* (Louisville: Westminster John Knox, 1989), 149.
4. Kathleen Fischer, *The Inner Rainbow: The Imagination in Christian Life* (New York: Paulist Press, 1983), 24.
5. Garret Green, *Imaging God: Theology and the Religious Imagination* (San Francisco: Harper & Row 1989), 94.
6. Eunjoo Mary Kim, *Preaching the Presence of God: A Homiletic from an Asian American Perspective* (Valley Forge: Judson, 1999), 117.
7. Fred. B. Craddock, *As One without Authority* (Nashville: Abingdon, 1971), 78.
8. Kim-Cragg, *Interdependence*, 7.
9. Homi Bhabha, *The Location of Culture* (New York: Routledge, 1994), 4.
10. Paul Scott Wilson, *Imagination of the Heart* (Nashville: Abingdon, 1988), 16.
11. Anna Carter Florence, "Preaching Imagination," in *Teaching Preaching as Christian Practice*, ed. Thomas Long and Leonora Tubbs Tisdale (Louisville: Westminster/John Knox, 2008), 123–124. The emphasis original.
12. Tom Troeger, "Can You Imagine This? The Future Role of Imagination in Preaching," in *Breaking on the Brink: The Future of Homiletics*, ed. Martha Simmons (Nashville: Abingdon, 1996), 136.
13. Wilson, *Imagination of the Heart*, 33.
14. Fumitaka Matsuoka, *Learning to Speak a New Tongue: Imagining a Way that Holds People Together-An Asian American Conversation* (Eugene: Pickwick, 2011), 132.
15. Walter Brueggemann, *The Practice of Prophetic Imagination: Preaching an Emancipatory Word* (Minneapolis: Fortress, 2012), 32.
16. Ibid., 6.
17. Mary Elizabeth Moore, *Teaching as a Sacramental Act* (Nashville: Abingdon, 2004), 193–194.
18. Brueggemann, *The Practice of Prophetic Imagination*, 3.
19. R. S. Sugirtharajah, *Postcolonial Reconfigurations* (St. Louis: Chalice Press, 2003), 8.
20. Kwok Pui-lan, "Postcolonial Preaching in Intercultural Contexts," *Homiletic* 40:1 (2015): 15.
21. Mary Donovan Turner, "Reversal of Fortune: The Performance of a Prophet," in *Performance in Preaching: Bringing Sermon to Life*, ed. Jana Childers and Clayton Schmit (Grand Rapids: Baker, 2008), 87–98.
22. Mary Hilkert, *Naming Grace: Preaching and the Sacramental Imagination* (New York: Continuum, 1997), 97.
23. Moore, *Teaching as a Sacramental Act*, 99.
24. Florence, *Preaching as Testimony*, 117.

25. Gayatri C. Spivak, *A Critique of Postcolonial Reason: Toward a History of the Vanishing Present* (Cambridge: Harvard University Press, 1999), 6.

26. Kwok, *Postcolonial Imagination*, 30.

27. Elizabeth Schüssler Fiorenza, *In Memory of Her: A Feminist Theological Reconstruction of Christian Origins* (New York: Crossroad, 1994), xxii.

28. Florence, *Preaching as Testimony*, 121.

29. Kwok, *Postcolonial Imagination and Feminist Theology*, 37.

30. Kwok, *Discovering the Bible in a Non-Biblical World* (Maryknoll: Orbis, 1995), 43.

31. Tat-siong Benny Liew, *What Is Asian American Biblical Hermeneutics? Reading the New Testament* (Honolulu: University of Hawai'i Press, 2008), 2, 19.

32. Stuart Hall, "When Was the 'Post-Colonial?' Thinking at the Limit," *The Post-Colonial Question: Common Skies, Divided Horizons*, ed. Iain Chambers and Lidia Curri (London: Routledge, 1996), 250.

33. Andrea Bieler, HyeRan Kim-Cragg, Isolde Karle, and Ilona Nord, eds., *Religion and Migration: Negotiating Hospitality, Agency and Vulnerability* (Leipzig: EVA, 2019); Susanna Snyder, Brazal, Agnes M., Ralston, Joshua, eds., *Church in an Age of Migration: A Moving Body* (New York: Palgrave, 2015).

34. James R. Nieman and Thomas G. Rogers, *Preaching to Every Pew: Cross-Cultural Strategies* (Minneapolis: Fortress, 2001).

35. Brueggemann, *The Practice of Prophetic Imagination*, 33.

Chapter 3

Place

Grappling with Colonial Realities and Locating One's Own Social Location

> *Now the Lord said to Abram, "Go from your country and your kindred and your father's house to the land that I will show you. I will make of you a great nation, and I will bless you, and make your name great, so that you will be a blessing. I will bless those who bless you, and the one who curses you I will curse; and in you all the families of the earth shall be blessed."*
>
> —Gen. 12:1–3

In the postcolonial world, the place of preaching is shifting and unstable. This is both a result of and a reaction to the rigid and binary colonial construction of nation, culture, and ideologies that have plagued the world and been challenged by the billions who suffer from it. This chapter affirms a postcolonial world that is characterized by "global complexity, geographical/geopolitical deterritorialization, and reterritorialization, border-crossings, threshold dwelling, transnationality, fluidity and hybridity."[1] Given these postcolonial characteristics, it is impossible for the preaching place to be a cozy or secure place. Rather, it must be a courageous place, locating itself within the postcolonial church that transgresses the status quo and transforms traditional practices. This courageous place of preaching is also a liminal space, a fleeting Kairos passage that is in between stable and transformative, confronting and comforting, excruciating and exhilarating, and lamenting and laughing.

In order to understand what I mean by the "place" of preaching in a postcolonial sense, it is necessary to engage several postcolonial concepts. As a way of discussing the role of place for postcolonial preaching, I will first map out North America as a settler-colonial state by examining immigration policy. To help us understand the nature of the preaching place and its potential as a location from which to share the good news, I will explore concepts such as Orientalism and mimicry, and examine the role of the trickster in postcolonial thought. Second, I make the case that postcolonial concepts are necessary for understanding the interlocking aspects of the various social locations in which preachers find themselves and for challenging preachers to engage the dynamics of postcolonial communication. I also suggest preaching strategies for postcolonial issues arising from migration contexts. Finally, a sermon is offered that highlights a postcolonial place.

NORTH AMERICA AS A COLONIAL PLACE

North America, or Turtle Island as indigenous people know it, has been shaped by European colonial conquest since at least 1492. During this colonial process, Christian preaching has positioned itself to privilege Anglo white elite men. Such a location was a direct result of the imposition of European colonial ways on others.[2] Eurocentric philosophy, culture, and language have shaped the place of preaching in North America.[3] Despite the fact that there are many preachers in North America today who do not conform to the gender, race, and language of the colonial norm, the preaching place today is still defined in terms of white male Anglo preachers. Critical analysis and serious engagement with the history of colonialism are, therefore, necessary to create a more inclusive and affirming place for a diversity of preachers. For this to take place or be realized, ethnicity, culture, race, and language must be taken seriously; as things that are inseparably intertwined with, and relevant to the discourse of the preaching place.

Modern colonialism was a European project in which the narrative of a racial hierarchy justified conquest and transatlantic slavery. Debra Mumford traces the very beginning of the West African slave trade and shows its close connection to the Christian civilizing mission. On June 18, 1452, Pope Nicholas V endorsed the Portuguese right to conquer and subjugate all the heathen, regarded as enemies of Christ. Portuguese colonialists further appealed to the pope for authorization not only to enslave West Coast Africans but also to sell them.[4] Because forced slavery and migration shaped North America, the discourse of place ultimately points to the fundamental question of "belonging." From the outset, for example, the North American colonies displaced indigenous people and used black slavery and racialized labor to develop its economy. The postcolonial discourse of place is a quest for finding a home for those who had to leave home, or a struggle to find refuge for those who lost home by force. In legal arenas, the notion of belonging is mostly associated with citizenship. Thus, the discourse of place is highly political in today's globalized society, where building walls and tightening borders between nation-states have recently become a theme of political speeches.

The notion of place as a home is a core biblical and theological concept. God summoned Abram and his family to leave home to find a home in a new place. In Genesis 12, God promises Abram and his family that after a period of migration, they and their descendants would be granted a place where they would belong. This divine promise is expansive and inclusive. "In you (Abram) all the families of the earth shall be blessed" (Gen. 12:4). There is no boundary of who is in and who is out in the home God has in mind. God is not saying that only the offspring of Abram will belong to God's place; in fact, at the time God said this to Abram, Abram had no offspring of his own.

Unfortunately, God's blessing to Abram (later Abraham) that "all the families of the earth will be blessed" has not been honored. God was adamant that those who curse others will be cursed. Yet we know that colonialism was a curse for many and that the colonial powers deployed a strategy whereby people were divided based on their culture, language, and skin color, using this division to mark some for privilege and others for slavery. The historical roots of racism are much more expansive in North America than the history of the slave trade alone. In fact, racism was an ideology developed by European colonial powers, which they based on pseudoscientific theories and applied broadly to the whole globe and all its people, dividing everyone into categories of humans and subcategories, implying a racial hierarchy. American studies scholar Lisa Lowe underscores that in addition to black slavery, Asian immigration to the United States was a key part of the racialized foundations of the United States.[5] Since 1850, Chinese, Japanese, and Filipinos were essential to the building of the railroads, the agricultural economy, and the textile and service industries in the United States. By 1880, however, the increase of a racialized labor population grew so large that it threatened the social position of white people. Thus, the state began to implement laws identifying citizenship with white people only, barring all immigrant groups from citizenship and ownership of property. Starting from 1882, people of Chinese origin were barred from citizenship, then in 1917 East Indians, in 1924 Japanese, and in 1934 Filipinos.[6]

A similar program of disenfranchisement was established in Canada. The Chinese Head tax passed into law in 1885 and effectively prevented the Chinese people from settling in Canada, even though they had worked hard to build the railroad that built the nation.[7]

Racist immigration policies were challenged in the twentieth century but attitudes remained deeply entrenched; and while policies changed, it was often simply a change in appearance with no fewer damaging consequences.

The 1965 immigrant act, which opened the way for migrants from Asia to enter and live in the United States, did not erase racism either. Despite a more inclusive immigration policy in 1965, the conditions of the undocumented immigrants from many places, including Mexico and Latin America, have not improved. Their exploited labors continue to be a significant part of the American economy to this day yet these migrants enjoy few rights or protections.

In Canada, up until the 1960s, immigration was much more difficult if you did not come from Europe, were not fluent in English or French, and were not Christian (better if you were Protestant and not Catholic or Orthodox Christian). Though they carried the same British Passport as Canadians, black and East Indian citizens of the Caribbean were barred from immigrating to Canada except under the strictest conditions.[8] Canada made changes to its racially biased immigration policy in 1965, the same year that the United States did. In 1971, it even went so far as to implement a so-called multiculturalism act, touted as the most inclusive immigration policy in the world.[9] This policy nonetheless concealed patterns of colonial racism.

The social movement of the 1960s and 1970s brought together migrants of Asian, African, Chicano-Latino descent, as well as Native Americans in the United States, to protest and speak out against the racialized society that oppressed them. Their voices challenged racial segregation and exposed the conditions of racialized laborers and economic exploitation. During these decades, race was the locus of struggle and was met with state violence. This revealed the constitutional contradiction of liberal democracy. Lowe puts it this way: "The promise of inclusion through citizenship and rights cannot resolve the material inequalities of racialized exploitation . . . . The demand for civil rights for racialized people heightened the contradictions inherent in the promise of universal equality."[10]

This brief review of immigration policy since the nineteenth century in the United States and Canada reveals the painful truth of colonial violence and racial discrimination, which were present in the very origins of both nations and continue to this day. Colonial realities linger on. Indeed, it is not wrong to say that slavery and chattel exploitation of racism have not ended, but continue in the postcolonial world as a kind of modern-day slavery.[11] The struggle against colonialism and white racism under the transnational capitalist economy and cultural imperialism is far from over. Postcolonial analysis is necessary, because it provides useful tools for understanding these structural sins and for articulating the role of preaching in this context. We will now work to make a link between postcolonial concepts and preaching contexts as a way of probing the place of the preacher in the postcolonial world.

ORIENTALISM

Orientalism is a discursive form of knowledge about the Orient, created by the Western imperial powers to establish asymmetrical relationships between the so-called Occident (itself) and the Orient (the colonized other). Where is the Occident or the Orient? This discursive strategy was revealed and introduced to academic scrutiny by the literary critic Edward Said.[12] According to Said, the Orient does not exist as a geographical place, even if that is what it implies. The Orient and the Occident are imaginative constructs, which serve a global hegemony. The discourse of Orientalism was created to maintain a hierarchical dichotomy between the colonialist and the colonized in the nineteenth century during the colonial expansion, creating a stark division between the colonized (nonwhite, non-Christian, not Europeans) as inferior and the colonialist (white, Christian, and Europeans) as superior. Those deemed to be of nonwhite-European descent, who were also often identified by the fact that they were non-Christian—namely Jews, Muslims, Pagans, and so forth, were represented as the people of the Orient. This diverse group was targeted, threatened, and exploited. This Orientalist prejudice and discrimination are operational in the era of global migration. While the modern colonialism of the territorial occupation has ended, the orientalizing attitudes and policies continue into the twenty-first century.

In this sense, we have not entered the "post" (after) colonial era.[13] The fact is that we still live in a heavily white-supremacist and orientalizing place. Racial tensions have arguably increased in recent years, thanks to recurring state-sponsored acts of discrimination, hate crimes, and shootings of ethnic minorities; especially black Americans and Hispanic Americans in the case of the United States, and Black and Indigenous peoples and People of Color (BIPOC) in Canada. There are too many of such acts to list. As I write these words, anger at the senseless death of George Floyd is still churning in the streets of North America and around the world. This is just the latest example, and more are coming to light every day; shockingly, but not surprisingly. These are undeniable signs that racialized people[14] continue to be targeted for violence in the current world order.

The history of black people in the United States is particularly instructive. Black populations in the United States have suffered most since they came to North America as slaves and victims of state-sanctioned terrorism, murder, brutality, and violence at the hands of authorities and vigilante individuals and groups. The Black Lives Matter movement is the most recent manifestation of resistance to this treatment. This movement began after an unarmed teenager Michael Brown was shot and killed by a police officer Darren Wilson, in Ferguson, Missouri. Wilson was acquitted of the charge of murder. Brown was only one of countless young black people, who fell victim to structural racism. The statement made by the Religious Education Association, the oldest academic association in North America, compiled a list of over 100 names; mostly of young black men, whose precious lives were taken by the principalities and powers of white supremacy in the United States.[15]

How, then, do we preach about and from this place? How can we unmask this violence on this land as an essential task of preaching? Is the very place from which we preach complicit in this violence? The concept of Orientalism is one idea that successfully unveils the invisible systematic violence embedded in race, language, culture, religion, and media. Biblical studies and Christian preaching are not immune from Orientalism's epistemic violence. According to the postcolonial thinkers such as Said, the biblical and theological language of European Christianity, which views itself as the standard of truth before, which other religious traditions fall short, is inseparably connected to the history of colonialism and imperialism.[16] The production of cultural and religious knowledge was presented to Western and non-Western people alike as an impartial and objective truth. Martin Bernal, following Said's work, demonstrates how the allegedly objective historical scholarship of the Classics was, in fact, determined by its own cultural and political history of racism and Eurocentrism.[17] The purportedly impartial objective study of Christian biblical criticism and Christian theology became the golden standard in homiletics. Proclaiming *the* objective and universal truth of the Gospel derived from Scripture prevailed for many centuries and was certainly prevalent in the building of the United States as a Christian nation.

The discourse of Orientalism takes on added meaning in the current context of displacement and migration. Postcolonial biblical scholar Fernando Segovia, when speaking of the experience of being colonized, uses the Spanish term, *arrojar*, which means "thrown" or even "vomited out."[18] It is a term that vividly and viscerally captures the painful experience of migration and the turbulent nature of this displacement imposed by colonization. For Gayatri C. Spivak, another postcolonial scholar, the postcolonial displacement is like having her home named by someone else. Displacement is about the process by which the name of places is given to colonized people by the colonizing power as a way to define and confine them.[19] Here she articulates the problem of representation.

Spivak's ideas are further worth pondering in terms of a preacher's power in representing others. From a preacher's perspective, Spivak reminds us that written histories about others, even the histories contained in our Bible, are problematic. The voice of those she calls subalterns, people who cannot speak for themselves, is by definition not included in written accounts of the past or present. Spivak points out that subalterns are often racialized and colonized women and asks if they could speak because they are already (mis)represented by the colonial power before they speak.[20] This presents an insoluble contradiction. One cannot rewrite colonial history without including those voices; which by definition are not part of the written history.[21] Preachers, then, must paradoxically hear the voices that are not heard, listen between the lines, outside the texts of the Bible, and inside the texts of history to hear what is really going on, even if their ability to do so is limited by their position. Postcolonial preachers must develop and raise awareness of the ways subaltern experiences are often assimilated into the experiences of those in power. They must work to decenter the colonial norm of the white male English-speaking preacher and combat the discourse of Orientalism.[22]

MIMICRY IN HYBRIDITY

Using a linguistic metaphor, mimicry indicates the ways the colonized imitate or learn to speak the language of the colonials. Its meaning in postcolonial discourse is not limited to speech, however, but extends to all aspects of culture and government. On the one hand, mimicry represents the erasure of the colonized's own identity. On the other hand, mimicry can be adopted as a tool of resistance to subvert the colonial power. Homi Bhabha, a postcolonial theorist, developed the idea of mimicry in a work entitled *Location of Culture*.[23] According to him, mimicry is always an imperfect copy. In their efforts to be like the colonizers, Bhabha quips that the colonized are often judged to be almost but not quite white colonizers. This reflects a perpetual and hopeless situation of being constantly judged to be inferior. However, it can also be a deliberate strategy on the part of the colonized to mock the colonizer and establish a difference that the colonized claims as their own.

Diane Taylor, a scholar on performance studies, provides an example of mimicry in the event of European missionaries trying to teach Mexican indigenous people about the Eucharist:

> The friars riled against any mixing and overlapping of belief systems 'until the heathen ceremonies and false cults of their counterfeit desires are extinguished, erased . . . . Insisting on strict orthodoxy, they feared anything in indigenous practice that somehow resembled or overlapped with their own. [And yet] Duran, in the *Book of God and Rites*, draws some uneasy comparisons between the Nahua's practice of human sacrifice and Christian communion, noting, 'how cleverly this diabolical rite imitates that of our Holy Church . . . Native peoples came to be seen as perpetual performers, engaged in "idolatrous dissembling . . . like monkeys, looking at everything, so as to imitate whatever they see peoples do." On the other hand, Europeans . . . had praised the native peoples' capacity for imitation and used that to argue that they could be taught to be Christians and take the sacrament. On the other hand, the mimicry was inappropriate.[24]

This mimicry, even if it is subtle, is subversive. It is subversive because mimicry enables the colonized to satisfy the colonial desire, behaving as if they could follow Christian teachings; yet, the very attempt to imitate them problematizes the legitimacy and superiority of the colonial teachings, and even mocks their teachings. On one hand, mimicry can be a devastating critique of colonized culture, which demands purity and detests the mixing of their own Christian practices with the colonized practices. On the other hand, mimicry as a hybrid performance is cunning because it is so subtle, the colonizer does not know if they are being flattered or made fun of.

TRICKSTER

The preaching place is amid climate change and global warming, which have been causing massive ecological migration. This fact reminds us that the pulpit and the congregation are part of and not set above creation. The natural world as an unpredictable and shifting place invites preachers to behold a homiletical horizon that is as wide as it is wild. Donna Haraway, who is a leading scholar in ecofeminism, speaks of creation's "witty agency."[25] For Haraway, nature is neither a static object nor a passive commodified resource for humans to extract and consume. Rather, it is an organic, ongoing, changeable, and unpredictable entity. Others speak of nature having wit as a trickster and emphasize its playfulness and cunningness. This trickster insight comes from indigenous wisdom, although "fools are everywhere."[26] Trickster stories often personify this aspect of nature in the character of a coyote or bird. Seeing creation as a trickster implies that creation has a power that is beyond human control. Creation can trick humans and expose human vulnerability and dependence.[27] Homileticians Charles Campbell and Johan Cilliers have the following to say about tricksters:

> [Trickster] will die, and then suddenly returns to life; go to the underworld, then return to the living. Tricksters live and function at the boundaries, regularly unmasking, crossing, and redefining those boundaries. They are figures on the margin, belonging to the periphery, not the center. As such, they are transgressive, disruptive figures.[28]

Catherine Keller, as a postcolonial theologian who has attended to the ecological crisis, makes the claim that nature as a trickster "not only subverts the grinding exploitation of the feminized earth, but supersedes the maternal altogether. Trickster 'makes room for some unsettling possibilities, including a sense of the world's independent sense of humor.'"[29]

Homiletician Leah Schade extends the notion of the trickster to Jesus. She is aware of the ecofeminists' uneasiness with regard to the resurrection of Jesus, which seems to be incompatible with the cycle of life in creation as well as the complaint that the resurrection had been interpreted as the male deity's usurping of the natural process of life and death. Yet, she nudges us to think of the resurrected Jesus as an event that surprises the conventional view of death and outwits the seemingly powerful androcentric forces that seek to dominate it. Schade makes a case that creation is sometimes victimized by the same forces that crucified Christ.[30] Surprises are what tricksters do best. In many ways, the cross and the resurrection of Jesus are the most scandalous theological surprises. The idea of the trickster can guide the preachers in their postcolonial reflections of the places where ecological and other related crises force the migrations of millions to leave their home. The concept of trickster enables them to lift up the often-unpredictable agency of God in subverting these forces.

SHIFTING SOCIAL LOCATIONS OF PREACHERS AND CONGREGATIONS

A key to effective preaching in the twenty-first century is an awareness of the differences that include, but are not limited to race, ethnicity, gender, and social location. This awareness makes the way people hear sermons. Dawn Ottoni-Wilhelm urges preachers to recognize the diversity of listener experiences. "[Not] all listeners will travel along a common trajectory set out by the preacher in a sermon."[31] She rightly points to a need to attend to listeners' different experiences and the roles these play in their reception of a sermon. However, she does not explicitly recognize the diverse experiences of the preachers themselves that impact sermon construction. In short, a self-critical examination of the preacher's own social locations and her/his/their privileges is as important as a critical examination of the social location of the people as listeners in the pew.

The close examination of and attention to preachers' own places become critical when diverse experiences in the pew and that in the pulpit are in conflict. When Ottoni-Wilhelm writes, "in our effort to identify with listeners and to speak with and to them, we may be assuming that we know much more than we actually know,"[32] it seems to assume that it is the preacher who alone is in a position to know and is in need of understanding those in the pew. But what of the responsibility of those in the pew to know the preacher? And what about the preacher's own self-knowledge? These are important postcolonial considerations as well. A preacher is positioned by the gaze of the congregation. That gaze, especially if it is the white gaze at the preacher who is racialized, needs to be disclosed and interrogated. The challenge in terms of addressing the preaching place of preachers who are non-normative in the colonial sense is growing. Many of these preachers serve predominantly white, middle-upper class, and English-speaking congregations.

The postcolonial place draws attention to the migration context, which complicates the relationship between preacher and congregation. Most congregations are still homogenous in mainline denominations, though this is changing. Sermons will need to address the diversity of the congregation and the context, which is bringing different cultures together. What is more, pulpits are increasingly going to be occupied by preachers who are new to the country and have different social, economic, and cultural backgrounds. In my experience, there are three types of situations that are increasingly prevalent in today's congregations. One situation is where a preacher who is not white and who is a recent immigrant serves a predominantly white settler congregation. In this type of congregation, there is often a struggle for the minister and congregation to understand one another. This is true in the literal sense that congregations of immigrant preachers, especially nonwhite immigrant preachers, will often complain that they cannot understand what is being said from the pulpit due to the preacher's non-normative accent. This is often experienced as a subtle (or not so subtle) manifestation of racism. On the other hand, the preacher is faced with the challenge of discerning the needs of a congregation with a very different set of assumptions and expectations from those congregations in the country from which the preacher came.

Another common type is the ethno-specific congregation where the preacher came from the same ethnic background as those in the congregation, but due to the long immigrant history of the congregation's ethnic group, the preacher is faced with a number of stark cultural differences. For example, the long-time members of the congregation may be accustomed to and expect the church to conform to the norms of the churches in the country from which they came at the time in which they left it. While the church culture may have changed significantly since then, these members may not be aware of or be able to relate to that change. More recent immigrants in the same congregation may not share their values. Additionally, the children of the earlier immigrant parents may not speak the language of their parents or grandparents. Their own culture and worldview may have been strongly influenced by the local culture. These three groups may identify with one another ethnically but culturally speaking they are different. Often these congregations are bilingual. They pose a unique set of challenges for preachers.

The third type of congregation, which is growing, is the type that is moving beyond the racially homogenous and monolingual status quo. These congregations are growing in racial and cultural diversity. The challenges faced in this situation center around developing new norms, accommodating new expressions of church, and honoring new forms of leadership. Diverse languages need to find a way of being expressed in worship. The racial inequalities of the dominant society (and of church culture itself) need to be addressed. Ways to share leadership and ownership need to be negotiated. Not only are cultures mixed in this situation, but entirely new cultures are birthed in the same way. Congregations that consist of various interracial families do not merely represent the coming together of different skin colors and cultures, but rather the emergence of a different skin color and culture altogether.

The three different types of the churches named here require preachers to develop homiletic models that adequately address the distinct places in which their congregations find themselves. It is necessary to find a preaching voice that is reflective of, and relevant to postcolonial migration contexts. Therein lies a promise and a new possibility of creating preaching places where the heterogeneous, unique, and marginal social locations of people and preachers are affirmed; and therein lies a practice of rehearsing the realm of God. To enhance this practice, given below are a couple of tips that help preachers create a postcolonial preaching place.

Preacher's Self-Study

Both white and nonwhite, Anglo and non-Anglo preachers need to be familiar with issues pertinent to race, ethnicity, and culture. If you are white, reading books that are written by nonwhite academics and homileticians would provide a healthy growing edge, though it is not always easy to find such books. By the same token, if you belong to an ethnic minority group, read books that are written specifically about ethnic and cultural issues that are different from your own. If you are of Asian descent, read books by Latinx and African American preachers and their congregations, for example.[33] Furthermore, it will be generative to pay attention to scholarship that takes an interdisciplinary approach. A siloed view of preaching may miss opportunities to see how all aspects of church life are interconnected and how issues connected to postcolonial contexts intersect. Finally, it is essential to read broadly from works that engage cultural differences, decolonization, and postcolonial biblical interpretation.[34]

In your own study, ask yourself the following questions: How would you describe your location as a preacher vis-à-vis ethnic, racial, and linguistic identity? In what ways does your social location influence how you interpret Scripture and deliver sermons? Have you thought of how your sermons may omit or mispresent certain ethnicities, racial, and cultural groups in the congregations? Have your sermons ever given offense, and how can you learn from this? Are your sermons, in terms of examples and implications, relevant to your and other's ethnic and cultural contexts? And in what ways could your sermons improve their approach to experiences of nonwhite, non-Anglo members?³⁵ These questions may lead a preacher to acknowledge a need for communal exegesis and sermon study. Self-reflective questions arising from preachers' self-study will contribute to wholesome cultural exegesis (both scriptural and contextual), underscoring the importance of people's social locations.

Pulpit as a Communal Preaching Place

Preaching is never a solitary act. It involves people; people from the congregation, people outside church, and even creation itself. Leonora Tisdale talks about "local theologies" emerging from folk art, and cultural wisdom carried by people in a specific place.³⁶ Excited and innovative local theologies are emerging in places of cultural, ethnic, and racial diversity. More than twenty years ago, there was a push by homileticians, such as John S. McClure and Lucy A. Rose, to involve congregations in the very process of sermon preparation, delivery, and evaluation.³⁷ It is encouraging to note that some schools with Doctor of Ministry preaching programs advocate that laypeople be involved in the development and preaching of the sermon. Millennials are encouraged to share their thoughts before and after the sermon is delivered.³⁸ Yet, the pulpit is still often solely occupied by a single preacher rather than being a participatory place involving diverse people. But as noted earlier, preaching is part of the liturgy and the "liturgy," etymologically speaking, means the work of the people, hence, preaching ought to be conducive to the work of the whole people of God. If this is not an explicit part of the process of sermon preparation, delivery, and evaluation, it should at least be the explicit intention of the preacher to draw on the congregation's experiences and insights.

SERMON EXAMPLE

I include a sermon below as an example of how I have addressed racism and ecological concerns in light of thinking from a postcolonial preaching place. This sermon was preached at the Annual Meeting of the Saskatchewan Conference of the United Church of Canada, Battlefords, Saskatchewan in 2018.

This sermon features a critical event that, like the death of George Floyd in 2020 in the United States, tore the mask off the systematic racism that exists in the Canadian justice system. In 2016, Colten Boushie, a young indigenous Cree man, was shot dead by Gerald Stanley, a white farmer, who was later acquitted on the charge of murder. This decision clearly revealed how white racism against indigenous people is sanctioned by the police and court system. Indigenous peoples and concerned non-indigenous citizens raised their voices in a loud outcry, and Canada experienced a moment of reckoning. It is still working through what it means for the nation and how to approach reconciliation with indigenous people; and it will have to continue to do so for generations.

I crafted this sermon ahead with the six RIPPLE principles in mind. Place was a particularly important consideration for the sermon, as the Annual Meeting for Saskatchewan Conference was held in the same town where the trial of Gerald Stanley had taken place. The sermon paints Jesus as a trickster, confronting sinful colonial complicity in a cunning way. Zacchaeus's repentance rippled through his community and continues to ripple through the life of the church in this time and place. The sermon offers another surprising actor in the story as well, the sycamore tree that Zacchaeus climbed, offering a new point of view on the Gospel.

"Humble like the Earth and Tall like a Tree"

Scripture: Luke 19:1–10

It is a blessing to be here together with you today, a large gathering of God's faithful people, in a beautiful place. Those of us who do not live in the Battlefords had to drive here over the big and wide rolling prairie of what used to be Canada's frontier, the great North-West Territories. We traveled beneath the living skies stretching from horizon to horizon in all four directions, under wispy white clouds like God's wings shelter us beneath the great blue heaven. All of us are in Treaty 6 land, which was brought into Canada through the covenant made with Cree, Saulteaux, and Dakota indigenous peoples in 1876. That covenant stated that the land would be shared for the benefit of both indigenous and settler communities. It is good to be here together in this blessed place.

The Creator has indeed blessed us in this place, but it is no longer the Garden of Eden it once promised to be. It has been riven by human strife and injustice. And all of us here this day are reeling from the events that have taken place in this community over the past two years. This past February (2018), after a trial that captivated and polarized the province, the nation, and the world, Gerald Stanley was found not guilty of second-degree murder in the 2016 shooting death of Colten Boushie. That decision took place at the Battlefords Court of Queen's Bench.

Many may be tempted to see the decision as an anomaly, as an isolated decision that does not reflect a long and systematic pattern of injustice in our nation's justice system. But let me share a story that may shake this conviction. Around 113 years ago, in this same place, there was another trial; a trial which was as divisive of indigenous and settler communities, as it was devastating for the indigenous people of this place. The Battlefords were the seat of government power in 1885 at the time of the Riel Uprising. At the time of the uprising, the famous chief Big Bear, Mistahimaskwa, was squatting just over the Alberta border in a place called Frog Lake. The Big Bear people were hungry. Not far from their encampment was a government store house full of food. The government agents, who were associated with the store houses were particularly cruel, and had also received orders to keep back food, which had been promised under the conditions of Treaty 6 to indigenous people in times of great need. When the young men of Mistahimaskwa's community could take it no longer, they vented their anger on the agent and other white settlers who got caught in the middle. Nine unarmed innocent settlers were killed. After the Riel Uprising had been put down the government hunted down Big Bear's people. Big Bear was sent to jail and was almost dead when he got out. Eight of his young men were also arrested. It was in a courthouse not far from here, that those eight members of Big Bear's people were tried for murder, as a result of the Frog Lake massacre. With historical distance, we can empathize with the loss of nine settlers. But we can also empathize with the feelings of desperation and rage as the young Cree men who watched their children and elderly people slowly starve to death while a government storehouse sat full of food. It was here in the Battlefords, that these eight indigenous people, including the son of the Chief Big Bear, were condemned to death. It was here that they were hanged, in what was to this day the largest mass execution in the history of Canada.

History does not repeat, but it can return. I'm afraid the painful history of the Battlefords continues to shape our society to this day, as we have just had another historic reckoning. These two trials in the place called the Battlefords have critical significance for the nation of Canada as a whole, as a colonial settler state. The Battlefords: rolling prairies, living skies, desperate struggles, brave crossings. The name of this place beckons us to remember the history. Today, I believe we are being called to confront that history. My history. Your history. Our history. How do we confront it? Scripture invites and illuminates.

As the preacher of the last Saskatchewan Conference before the church changes its governance structure, I chose the biblical text about Zacchaeus because the theme for the conference was "Be Brave, Be Bold and Stand Tall!" The last phrase "stood out" for me. Why? I guess no one noticed I'm just a little over five feet! I even wondered, is that why I was invited? Regardless, I took the liberty to choose an appropriate Bible passage: the story of Zacchaeus.

There are many interesting biblical figures but there are very few, and maybe only one, that was explicitly described as short in stature in the Bible. Zacchaeus and I have something in common: We are both close to the earth, but we do our best to stand tall!

Zacchaeus's story is well-loved across generations. It is a powerful story that challenges us to give up privilege, to share our wealth and to repent! That makes an important story, not just for me, but for us all.

It is also a story that excites children. Children can relate to being short and climbing trees. Indeed, it makes many of us smile at the thought of the bold and child-like way the wealthy Zacchaeus climbed a tree to see Jesus. However, people didn't laugh or smile at Zacchaeus. Rather they were angry. "Hey," they complained, "that short rich guy is jumping the queue, again! That dirty tax collector even got Jesus to come to his house when we have been waiting here all day just to get a glimpse of him."

People "muttered," the NIV version of the Bible says. They "grumbled," according to the NRSV version. As these two verbs indicated, people were complaining about Zacchaeus, but not strongly, not vocally, and certainly not in public. Zacchaeus had the Roman Empire's power on his back, so it was dangerous and unsafe for the crowd to protest too loudly about him. As you know, tax collectors were part of the colonial system, serving the Roman Empire. Here was Zacchaeus, complicit in the system, benefiting from the system, abusing the system again! The complaints were also toward Jesus, who seemed to endorse his power and even favor Zacchaeus's greedy life. But Jesus was no sucker. "Hey Zacchaeus! Let's go see your house, the one you bought with all that tax money you took from poor peasants." Because Jesus made a risky move of telling everyone there that he would stay at "the sinner's house," the truth of Zacchaeus, the life of the tax collector was made even more obvious. The generosity of Jesus toward Zacchaeus might have been a clever trickster way of pointing out his guilt, amplifying the crowd's muttering and grumbling. But the story did not end there. There was a most dramatic turn waiting to happen. Zacchaeus did not languish in his shame after what Jesus said to him but instead the Bible says, "Zacchaeus stood there."

Zacchaeus came down and stood! Zacchaeus stood up. Zacchaeus stood tall. And standing there in that moment he promised Jesus and all in earshot that he would change, he would give up half of his possession to share with the poor. And if he has cheated anybody, he would repay them four times over.

This is totally unexpected. Jesus never asked him to do this. The crowd had not demanded this, either. According to the rabbinic law, if a man confessed his guilt, he was not necessarily required to pay anything. Yet, why did Zacchaeus do this? Where is this bold and brave act of repentance coming from? What was the source of grace that surprised people who witnessed this act of repentance and still surprises us today?

William Shakespeare once wrote:

The quality of mercy is not strained;
It droppeth as the gentle rain from heaven
Upon the place beneath. It is twice blest;

It blesseth him that gives and him that takes:

Repentance is the same. It cannot be forced or imposed. It must be voluntary. It must come from a willing heart. And it must also be graciously accepted, or it is not entirely effective. Jesus helped Zacchaeus realize what he had done. But Jesus did not command Zacchaeus to repent. I suppose Jesus may have been surprised, too, as we are sometimes surprised by the first drops of rain in a storm! Are we ready to be surprised again?

This powerful story of repentance gives us hope for our own story. The story of the Battlefords, the execution of the Chief Big Bear's son, and seven other young men must be remembered. It must be pointed out, even as Jesus slyly pointed out Zacchaeus's wealth. The Stanley trial also points to that history of brokenness and reminds us of the mutual suffering we have experienced. But beyond remembering and pointing out what can we do? Can we demand repentance? Can we demand mercy? Perhaps. Perhaps not. Perhaps the only recourse is to continue remembering and waiting, somewhat akin to the way the dry earth waits and thirsts for rain that droppeth from above. To retell these stories is to look heavenward, and pant for the showers of God's mercy and justice. It is to wait on repentance with anticipation for healing. This waiting requires a communal effort. Waiting alone without knowing the future is hard work. Waiting together can build expectation. Repentance as rehearsal involves admitting one's own brokenness, owning our wrongdoings, waiting for justice and repentance together as a daily practice. It is about making ourselves like the earth, low and humble like the thirsty prairie soil.

Now there is a part of the story about Zacchaeus that is often overlooked, I think. And that is the sycamore fig tree. Is it possible to see and imagine the Grace of God in the tree?

Let me offer my musings on this tree.

Much of significance, albeit unnoticed, can be drawn to the tree that Zacchaeus climbed. It is a large evergreen tree with large, low branches. It is a perfect tree to climb for short people like Zacchaeus. This tree also produces figs multiple times a year. It is a generous tree: in the time of Jesus, the poor and the colonized would have come and eaten from the tree when they couldn't find anything else. It was an accessible and generous tree. It was a tree of grace, mercy, and justice.

Throughout the Bible, we find many references to trees. From the beginning of the Bible in Genesis, we learn of the tree of the knowledge, the original fruit tree in the Garden of Eden from which Eve and Adam ate. We find such a tree at the end of the Bible, as well, in Revelation, in the city of God, standing in the new city. Blessed are those who trust in God, says the psalmist, they will be like a tree planted by streams of water that bears its fruit in abundance. Jesus spoke of trees growing from tiny seeds that spread out to provide shelter for all within its branches.

The tree in the story of Zacchaeus is the source of multiple experiences of grace. This tree did not judge Zacchaeus because he was a tax collector. This tree did not refuse to be climbed by this jaded man. This evergreen tree stood tall at the crossroads where Zacchaeus and Jesus met. It provided the place of encounter and that of repentance.

Botanists teach us that sycamore trees grow where water is scarce.

God knows that as Christians, too, we will face challenges. Spiritual water is scarce on the prairies. The process of reconciliation between indigenous and non-indigenous people is slow. The decolonizing journey is bumpy. We, as the United Church of Canada, struggle to know what to do. God, through the sycamore tree, teaches us how we can grow in the dry soil even when the water seems hard to come by: standing still, standing strong, and standing tall, waiting patiently, gracefully, and mercifully.

I think of another tree. One that stood on Golgotha. And of eight more, the gallows where eight indigenous men were hung. The shadows from these trees fall across the land, from the Battlefords, to Ottawa and across the globe wherever there is brokenness, injustice, and conflict. It is a shadow of sin, but also an invitation to grace.

God is often found in the unexpected places and comes to us at an unplanned Kairos time. Like the sycamore fig tree, God's presence is evergreen, and everlasting. God's self-giving love bears fruit that is accessible, generous, merciful, and just.

Let us learn from Zacchaeus. Let us learn from the crowd. Let us make noises. Let us grumble and complain. Let us live close to the earth of repentance. Let us also look up to the tree and stand! Stand up with arms outstretched, ready to receive something from heaven.

Stand strong with roots planted and ready to drink any drop of mercy we are offered. Stand for a new history, imagine a new future, and greet a realm of God in the grace of the Holy, who calls us to be "humble like the Earth and stand tall like a tree."

NOTES

1. Eleazar Fernandez, "The Geopolitical and the Glocal: Situating Global Theological Voices in Theological Education," in *Teaching Global Theologies:*

Power and Praxis, ed. Kwok Pui-lan, Cecelia Gonzalez-Andrieu, and Dwight N. Hopkins (Waco: Baylor University, 2015), 173.

2. Debra J. Mumford, "Slavery Prosperity Gospel," *Homiletic* 41:1 (2016): 32.

3. Milton Gordon, *Assimilation in American Life: The Role of Race, Religion, and National Origin* (New York: Oxford University Press, 1964), 85.

4. Mumford, "Slavery Prosperity Gospel," 31.

5. Lisa Lowe, *Immigration Act: On Asian American Cultural Politics* (Durham: Duke University Press, 1996), ix.

6. Ibid., 13.

7. Kim-Cragg, *Interdependence*, 110.

8. Cecil Foster, *They Call Me George: The Untold Story of Black Train Porters and the Birth of Modern Canada* (Winsor: Biblioasis, 2019).

9. Kim-Cragg, *Interdependence*, 115.

10. Lowe, *Immigration Act*, 23.

11. W. Kurt Hauser, *Invisible Slaves: The Victims and Perpetrators of Modern-Day Slavery* (Stanford: Stanford University Hoover Institution Press, 2017).

12. Edward Said, *Orientalism* (New York: Knopf, 1978).

13. The concept of postcolonialism is always used with a sense of this irony. Though formal colonial arrangements have been dissolved, new forms of colonialism have replaced them. It is these forms of neocolonialism, which postcolonial thinkers grapple with.

14. I used this term "racialized" instead of people of color or nonwhite people because the latter term centers whiteness and makes whiteness invisible as if white people do not have skin colors.

15. https://religiouseducation.net/blog/archives/5879, accessed June 8, 2020.

16. Said, *Orientalism*.

17. Martin Bernal, *Black Athena: Afroasiatic Roots of Classical Civilization Vol I: The Fabrication of Ancient Greece 1785–1985* (London: Free Association Books, 1987).

18. Fernando F. Segovia, "And They Began to Speak in Other Tongues," in *Reading from This Place: Social Location and Biblical Interpretation in the United States, Vol. 1*, ed. Fernando F. Segovia and Mary Ann Tolbert (Minneapolis: Fortress, 1995), 3.

19. Gayatri Chakravorty Spivak, "The Post-Colonial Critic," in *The Post-Colonial Critic: Interviews, Strategies, Dialogues*, ed. S. Harasym (New York: Routledge, 1990), 68.

20. Gayatri Chakravorty Spivak, "Can the Subaltern Speak?" in *Marxism and the Interpretation of Culture*, ed. Cary Nelson and Lawrence Grossberg (Urbana: University of Illinois Press, 1988), 296–297.

21. Gayatri Chakravorty Spivak, *In Other Worlds: Essays in Cultural Politics* (New York: Methuen, 1987); *Outside in the Teaching Machine* (New York: Routledge, 1993).

22. John McClure, *Other-wise Preaching: A Postmodern Ethic for Homiletics* (St. Louis: Chalice, 2001), 49.

23. Bhabha, *Location of Culture*.

24. Diane Taylor, *The Archives and the Repertoire: Performing Cultural Memory in the Americas* (Durham: Duke University Press, 2003), 45.

25. Donna Haraway, "The Promises of Monsters: A Regenerative Politics for Inappropriate/d Others," in *Cultural Studies*, ed. Lawrence Grossberg, Gary Nelson, Paul Treichler (New York: Routledge, 1992), 297 (295–337). See also Michael E. Zimmerman, *Contesting Earth's Future: Radical Ecology and Postmodernity* (Berkeley: University of California Press, 1994), 364.

26. Beatrice Otto, *Fools Are Everywhere: The Court Jester around the World* (Chicago: University of Chicago, 2001).

27. Leah E. Schade, *Creation-Crisis Preaching: Ecology, Theology, and the Pulpit* (St. Louis: Chalice, 2015), 142.

28. Charles L. Campbell and Johan H. Cilliers, *Preaching Fools: The Gospel as a Rhetoric of Folly* (Waco: Baylor University Press, 2012), 71.

29. Catherine Keller, *Face of the Deep: A Theology of Becoming* (New York: Routledge, 2003), 192.

30. Schade, *Creation-Crisis Preaching*, 134–143.

31. Dawn Ottoni-Wilhelm, "New Hermeneutic, New Homiletic, and New Directions: An U.S.–North American Perspective," *Homiletic* 35:1 (2010): 27.

32. Ibid.

33. For example, Woosung Calvin Choi, *Preaching to Multiethnic Congregation: Positive Marginality as a Homiletical Paradigm* (New York: Peter Lang, 2015). Gonzales, Justo and Pablo Jiménez, *Pulpito* (Nashville: Abingdon Press, 2005). Kenneth G. Davis and Jorge L. Presmanes, eds., *Preaching and Culture in Latino Congregations* (Chicago: Liturgy Training, 2000). Cleophus J. LaRue, *The Heart of Black Preaching* (Westminster/John Knox Press, 2005); Kim, *Preaching the Presence of God.*

34. For example, Sara Ahmed, *Strange Encounters: Embodied Others in Post-Coloniality* (New York: Routledge, 2000), R. S. Sugirtharajah, ed., *The Vernacular Hermeneutics: The Bible and Postcolonialism 2* (Sheffield, 1999) Randall Bailey, Benny Liew, and F. Segovia, eds. *They Were All Together in One Place? Toward Minority Biblical Criticism* (Atlanta: Society of Biblical Literature, 2009), Kwok Pui-lan, *Postcolonial Imagination and Feminist Theology, Discovering the Bible in a Non-Biblical World*, Catherine Keller, et al., eds., *Postcolonial Theologies*, Nestor Medina, Alison Hari-Singh, and HyeRan Kim-Cragg, eds., *Reading in Between: How Minoritized Cultural Communities Interpret the Bible in Canada* (Eugene: Pickwick, 2019).

35. These questions are modified from Matthew D. Kim, "The World of Ethnic and Cultural Issues in Preaching," in *The Worlds of the Preacher: Navigating Biblical, Cultural, and Personal Contexts*, ed. Scott M. Gibson (Grand Rapids: Baylor, 2018), 83–84.

36. Leonora Tubbs Tisdale, *Preaching as Local Theology and Folk Art* (Minneapolis: Fortress, 1997).

37. McClure, *The Roundtable Pulpit* and Lucy Rose, *Sharing the Word: Preaching in the Roundtable Church* (Louisville: Westminster John Knox, 1997).

38. Frank Thomas, "The Truth Is Always Relevant: Race and Economics in Contemporary African American Preaching," *Homiletic* 41:1 (2016): 53.

Chapter 4

Pattern

Vessels to Carry the Living Water

The woman said to him, "Sir, you have no bucket, and the well is deep. Where do you get that living water?"

—John 4:11

The woman from Samaria in the Gospel of John asked Jesus questions, which led to a conversation of great theological, liturgical, and soteriological import.[1] The conversation between Jesus and the woman at the well is an example of a distinct pattern of speech and communication that prompts curiosity from contemporary preachers and holds clues about how to craft a sermon. This conversation that Jesus had with the Samaritan woman at the well is the longest one recorded among all four Gospels. This conversation, especially the woman's questions, also holds clues for a postcolonial preaching pattern.[2] The question of where we get that water is not just asking about the source, but about the method by which we get water, the message of the Gospel, metaphorically speaking. This has been a central question of preachers for many centuries and leads us to a discussion about preaching patterns. Postcolonial preaching is concerned with the same question.

A postcolonial preaching pattern seeks a method of drawing water, which is consistent with the source of the water itself. In other words, the how and the what of the message must work together. This is always the case, but it is particularly important in the postcolonial context where the old patterns for delivering a sermon run the risk of undermining the message. A pattern that relies on a rigid understanding of truth and authority, for example, will obviously not work in an environment where the new kinds of interactions between people of different places and culture make it obvious that congregations and preachers have a lot to learn from and about one another and where colonial patterns of hierarchical authority are being dismantled.

The chapter examines various patterns for preaching. As is the approach in the rest of the book, it will highlight the way postcolonial ideas ripple into the discipline of homiletics, applying a critical lens and giving new energy to heretofore established patterns of preaching. Along with deductive and inductive patterns, other distinguishable patterns from feminist, Asian, African American, and Latinx perspectives will be reviewed. The goal of this chapter is to review these various patterns, highlighting strengths and limitations, rather than opting for one over the others. The connections between these different patterns will be explored as well as their similarities and differences. Distinguishing each pattern is not to compartmentalize them. This is a basic principle of postcolonial thought, which pays attention to complexities, interrelatedness, as well as heterogeneity, and uniqueness in different ideas and approaches.

One of the most influential North American homiletical books that discusses forms of sermon is *Design for Preaching*. The author H. Grady Davis begins with this sweeping claim: "All life, every living thing we know, comes in some organic form.... We cannot have a thought without its form."[3] Any life-giving and life-saving idea, including the Christian message, must have a shape. The best metaphor for this organic form of preaching for Davis is a tree. "A sermon should be like a tree," as he writes like a poem,

It should be a living organism:
   With one sturdy thought like a single-stem
   With natural limbs reaching up into the light.
It should have deep roots:
   As much unseen as above the surface
   Roots spreading as widely as its branches spread
   Roots deep underground.
      In the subsoil of life's struggle.
      In the soil of the eternal Word."[4]

The idea that the sermon is like a tree was not Davis's original idea. This insight has been passed down from medieval times when the world was understood as an organic living breathing creation of God.[5] Tapping into this ancient wisdom, Davis's main insight is to think of the sermon content and form organically and relationally when designing a sermon. Davis recovered the medieval view of sermons as living organisms and reintroduced it in the mid-twentieth century to ignite a discussion about sermon design.[6] What Davis and other homileticians of the twentieth century have taught twenty-first preachers is that content and form must be integrated holistically, rather than regarded mechanically. Patterns, therefore, are part of an organic whole. Thus, in homiletics, the message and the method for delivering it are intricately connected. The content and the pattern of preaching are like hands that clap together to make a joyful noise to praise God.

PURITAN PLAIN AND EXPOSITORY PATTERNS

Propositional sermons using puritan and expository patterns are logical and linear. It normally begins with a main statement and ends with an application. Once a central concept as a general idea is established, it moves to the second step explaining that main message with relevant examples, followed by a concrete application, and ending with a final point. That is why a sermon with the puritan plain style is often called a "three-point sermon." This pattern, like the sermon as a tree metaphor, is a millennium-old method that arose from the *artes praedicanid* (art of preaching) manual during the medieval period.[7]

Unlike many critiques of the puritan plain and expository patterns as dry, lifeless, inflexible, and downright boring, the original vision of the deductive method was organic, alive, expansive, and appealing. This counterpoint can be well substantiated through an appreciation of the non-dualistic nature of medieval theology. In fact, some notable theologians including Hildegard of Bingen and Thomas Aquinas had a worldview that the earth was alive, and humans were part of, not above, the vital organic whole. The world, to them, was the marvelous design of God the creator.[8] With this worldview, a tree would be an appropriate metaphor for a sermon, underscoring the organic nature of the sermonic process.[9]

This organic view of the world and of the sermon was, however, shattered during the Enlightenment era, when people tended to see the world as mechanical rather than organic. Human reason was highlighted as the ultimate measure of knowledge. Preaching influenced by this modernist world view became rigid and lost its organic vitality. Dave Bland traces this loss back to Peter Ramus (1515–1572) who turned organic rhetorical patterns of sermons into "a fixed, mechanized system of logic,"[10] which then was picked up by the Puritan movement, which used it as method for converting heathens. Historically, as a method for converting others, this puritan plain pattern was reinforced by the forces of colonialism that sought to assimilate or obliterate the cultural other. This is where the deductive pattern becomes destructive and dangerous from the postcolonial perspective.

As we pointed out earlier, the puritan plain style of preaching normally follows three steps: (1) exegeting scripture, (2) identifying the doctrine from it, (3) applying it to the life of the congregation.[11] Following this pattern, the preacher's job is to articulate the precepts of the faith in a logical manner.

This style of sermon sees itself within the narrow bounds of trying to extrapolate a spiritual truth from scripture by means of reason.[12] In the expository patterns, scripture, as an absolute authority, is set on the highest pedestal. The sermon seeks to communicate the logical, objective, and universal truth from the Bible. Any emotional and subjective references in the exegetical process are to be avoided. Therapeutic and personalized preaching styles are strictly discouraged because the message would then rely on fallible and sinful human emotions including the preacher's own.

As the expository pattern normally puts emphasis on the authority of the Bible, it also assumes the authority of the preacher and the preacher's teaching office. But it is scripture that ultimately authorizes the preacher's message.[13] Expository sermons using the deductive pattern normally pursue a single biblical thought, whether that means choosing one word, one verse, or one book in the Bible. The preacher helps the congregation clarify the significance of the given passage or word and discern the meaning in the text. The job of the preacher is to embrace this single thought and organize it deductively so that the congregation does not get confused or lost in the middle of the sermon. The preacher unambiguously lays out this thought at the beginning and then unpacks the text.

There are obvious shortcomings in expository and deductive approaches from postcolonial perspectives as raised earlier. However, these patterns are not to be discarded off hand. A postcolonial approach to the pulpit entertains ambivalent and even contradictory homiletic patterns and avoids categorizing any patterns as if they are all good or all bad. The strength of the deductive expository patterns encourages preachers to wrestle with the text, especially when the text is not the one they would have chosen themselves. This pattern also addresses the issue of biblical and theological illiteracy,[14] a problem that is increasingly urgent for twenty-first-century Christians.

INDUCTIVE AND NARRATIVE PATTERNS

The introduction of the inductive approach to preaching fifty years ago was a response to what many preachers felt were shortcomings in the deductive approach. Fred Craddock, in his book *One without Authority*,[15] explains the basics of the inductive approach. Rather than seeking definitive conclusions and irrefutable truths based on first principles, the inductive sermon pattern involves surprises, new discoveries, or open possibilities.[16] It is not the job of the inductive sermon to summarize and define something for the listeners, but to honor the way a congregation will be able to come to their own conclusions and wrestle with unresolved questions. Inductive sermons aim not to give a definite answer but to provide an experience. That is why inductive preaching becomes a "listening event."[17] Its purpose includes evoking the congregations' experiences as they encounter events in the Bible. The inductive sermon provides a journey. On that journey, the congregation experiences ups and downs, twists and turns, suspense and surprises. Eugene Lowry describes the journey in terms of different audience reactions: "oops, ugh, aha, whee, and yeah."[18] When preachers using the inductive pattern encounter the biblical text, they do not presume to know what it means right away. Instead, preachers search for its meaning by scouring for clues, comparing other texts, reading other commentaries, and using imagination. They may (or may not) find some illuminating insights to share with the congregation; but preachers, through the inductive approach to preaching, can guide the congregation to enter their own search.

The emphasis on the process or the journey rather than the destination is the strength and the weakness of inductive preaching. It creates a creative space where both the preacher and the congregation take a journey together. Yet, because it does not have a clear map, the journey can go astray. The other problem with inductive preaching is that it may assume too much of the people in the pew, who may not be adequately equipped for the journey. What is more, an uncritical reading of the text combined with an overreliance on human experiences may expose the sermon to the risk that it will be manipulated by the preacher or the audience to their own selfish ends.[19]

The inductive preaching pattern assumes that people have the capacity to follow an intellectual, literary, and often ambiguous path to understanding. This pattern requires biblical literacy and theological aptitude of the congregation. Yet many people in the church today live in a biblically and theologically illiterate world. Some are influenced by fundamentalist and literalist views of the Bible. The Book of Revelation, for example, has been interpreted by millions of Christians in a way that is dangerous and destructive. Lost on many is the context of the early Christians whose experiences and insights gave rise to this book. This addresses specifically their confrontation with worldly power; as they resisted the monstrous Roman Empire, denounced its hegemony, and consequently suffered exile, and yet remained steadfast in announcing the Divine victory.[20] Despite its importance, Ron Allen names a few reasons why preachers avoid the Book of Revelation: its obscurity and unintelligibility, the lectionary's minimizing treatment of the book, and the popular apocalyptic influence featured in the Left Behind series, created by Tim LaHaye and Jerry Jenkins.[21] Does the inductive method of preaching provide the tools needed to combat both such abuses and the unhelpful avoidance of certain texts in scripture? It may be irresponsible for preachers to rely on experiences to provide the congregation who may (or may not) have the proper understanding of texts, such as Revelation. To some extent, the strength of the deductive and expository patterns is the weakness of the inductive pattern, which takes for granted the congregation's biblical and theological literacy. This becomes even more dangerous when the text is difficult, filled with apocalyptic images, violence, and judgmental punishments. The preacher using the inductive pattern still needs to have a direction, or an anchor, even if it is provisional.

There are positive contributions to inductive patterns of preaching, albeit its potential weakness. Using the inductive pattern, the realities of people's lives (especially marginalized experiences) can be lifted up rather than buried under propositions, as is the danger with the deductive pattern. Wilson notes that the inductive pattern, as part of the New Homiletic movement, arose in the era of the Vietnam War, and the death of God movement when the authority of institutional religions and governments were being contested and challenged.[22] Contextual theologies such as liberation theology and feminist theology arose at the same time, while interest in human rights, civil rights, and the realities of various marginalized groups became the focus of public discussion. Under the umbrella of the New Homiletic movement, inductive sermons could help people to effectively identify themselves with people in the Bible, especially the marginalized, whose experiences became integral to shaping the message.

In summary, while the deductive expository pattern embraces propositional, preacher-centered, logical, argumentative, definite, objective, and didactic preaching, the inductive pattern is often used in imaginative, narrative, listener-centered, suggestive, open-ended, subjective, and invitational preaching. Both patterns have strengths and weaknesses, as there is no "one-size-fits-all" approach to preaching. While both patterns have been treated as if they are in a tug of war, a suggestion from a postcolonial perspective is to use them in creative tension. In most cases, sermons actually mix these two seemingly opposite approaches, incorporating other patterns as well. Being able to navigate differences and hold them in tension together is key to a postcolonial pattern of preaching.

As we have examined two general and dominant preaching patterns, let us now move on to patterns arising from specific social and cultural locations. We will start with a feminist preaching pattern and move through Asian, African American, and Latinx patterns. Of course, there is no one essential pattern for any of these approaches. For the sake of simplicity and clarity, however, the discussion of each different preaching pattern will highlight one representative scholar, who has articulated the shape of the sermon from their community's perspective. After we have explored these different patterns, we will briefly bring them into conversation to compare their similarities and differences, and what we can learn from them.

A FEMINIST PREACHING PATTERN

By feminist preaching, we mean a "religious proclamation that seeks to address the oppression, violence, and inequity created by the social reality of gender injustice."[23] Thus, the goal of a feminist preaching pattern is to reinforce "preaching practices designed to overcome gender oppression and injustice."[24] Here I feature feminist homiletics scholar Christine Smith as one of the first to propose a feminist preaching pattern. She offers four principles of sermon design for feminist preaching: (1) proportion, (2) balance, (3) emphasis, and (4) rhythm.[25] These principles are drawn from the art of weaving.[26] Smith argues that a pattern of feminist preaching involves "an ordered arrangement of parts that make a whole."[27] This concern for wholeness resonates with the call for "organic unity" in a sermon that was discussed earlier regarding Davis's comparison of the sermon to a tree, a comparison dating back to the medieval era. This holistic and organic pattern aims to "bring the sermon to life."[28]

Proportion

Proportion as the first movement in a feminist pattern is a kind of measurement. It involves a decision about how much or how little time will be allocated to each section in a sermon. Smith insists that the beginning of the sermon must include women's experiences and their lived reality. In this respect, Smith's choice of weaving as a metaphor for a feminist preaching pattern makes sense because weaving is one of the most prevalent kinds of work of the ordinary and marginalized women across the globe. This highlights the priority of women's experiences in feminist preaching. Smith writes, "Women's deepest and most profound experiences of faith, of relationality, of God and of incarnation have not been named" in traditional forms of preaching that have dominated for many centuries.[29] This metaphor of proportion makes two important points. First, measuring women's experience matters, in terms of having a proportion of that experience included in the sermon. Second, simply including experiences as an example is insufficient. Rather, the experiences of women that expose sexism as much as their resilience and resistance against it must always be central to shape the very form of the sermon.

Balance

Balance as the second feminist sermon design seeks to create a state of equilibrium. A goal of feminist preaching is to transform existing oppressive traditions by challenging patriarchal and sexist practices, but its goal is not to destroy or discard all traditions. Balancing between old and new is essential to feminist preaching. Smith alludes to the warp and weft of the weaving process in explaining what she means by balance. She asserts that "the durable warp [tradition and its critique] strands give substance and shape to the weft [possibility or vision] strands that show forth."[30] Feminist preaching is aware of the importance of tradition because it provides important structure. Despite the difficulty of facing and embracing traditions steeped in patriarchy and oppression, and the temptation to simply discard them, proclaiming the Gospel requires the feminist preacher to walk a fine line between these two extremes like a tightrope walker or a fiddler on a roof. In this regard, a feminist preaching pattern is interested in reconstruction rather than creating out of nothing. The emphasis on reconstruction shares an insight of postcolonial thought. Even if there is a desire to return to a precolonial world without colonial conquest and violence, we cannot. The world as we know it today is shaped by it and will never be the same. In the same way, even if we long to go back to the pre-patriarchal world, we cannot. The world as we know it is shaped by patriarchy. But we can overcome it and reconstruct it through rehearsing the realm of God.

Emphasis

Emphasis in the art of weaving determines what stands out and captures our attention. Size, color, or texture is used for doing the emphasis, catching the eye. In the art of preaching, catching the eye or the ear is done through the work of imagination. Feminist homileticians Mary Donovan Turner and Mary Lin Hudson emphasize imagination along with "listening and naming" as key to feminist homiletics.[31] In the interviews of feminist homiletics professors, Smith discovered two different emphases that they highlight in preaching: (1) women reveal much more of themselves in preaching than men; (2) women tend to use imagination more than men.[32] The self-revelation indicates that feminist preaching is relational; emphasizing less hierarchical and more egalitarian relationships through the preaching act. To accomplish that emphasis, the preacher takes a risk of being vulnerable.

Rhythm

Smith explains that in the art of weaving, rhythm is "a sense of continuity or recurrence, a succession of spaced intervals. In a visual design, rhythm causes the eye to travel from one part of the composition to another until the entire work has been perceived."[33] A feminist pattern is essentially like listening to one's own heartbeat, or its rhythm of life. Here, rhythm is a fundamental part of our innermost selves, finding one's call or her purpose in life. Finding one's vocation is never done; it takes a whole life span. A feminist sermon that helps to find one's vocation moves the congregation beyond the immediate present toward a future that is just about to be created. In this regard, feminist preaching is eschatological. As every Sunday is a little Easter, every sermon is a part of the bigger proclamation of the Good News, following the paschal mystery of the life, suffering, death, and resurrection of Jesus, and a salvific design of God the creator. In this sense, feminist sermonic movement is imbued with the rhythm of the incarnation.

AN ASIAN PREACHING PATTERN

Eunjoo Mary Kim's work helps us to articulate an Asian preaching pattern.[34] Before examining this form, however, it should be said that Asia is the most religiously and culturally pluralistic continent in the world. Thus, to propose an Asian sermonic pattern is not to foreclose the existence of other Asian patterns. Kim's approach focuses on East North Asia—Korea, Japan, and China—where Buddhism and Confucianism have had a significant impact for thousands of years and continue to influence people's lives, including the lives of Christians who live there today. Of course, even within this region, there is significant diversity. Also, there are many diasporas from these regions in North America and around the world. This introduction of an Asian preaching pattern will not essentialize Asia of Asian-ness but merely suggests an important aspect.[35]

Kim presents four characteristics of an Asian preaching pattern developed out of Confucian and Buddhist traditions: (1) holistic knowing, (2) the pursuit of consensus, (3) the dialogue of silence, and (4) indirect communication. They function in a spiral fashion. The pattern with these characteristics is like a thought process turning in on itself even as it moves downward. In a spiral sermon pattern, one can imagine a central theme like a gravitational pull drawing a sermon inward.[36] The central theme is not always at the end, as in inductive and narrative patterns of a sermon. It is not necessarily placed at the beginning either, as in the case of the deductive propositional expository pattern of preaching. Each cycle of the spiral feels the pull of slowly approaching the theme but may never actually reach the end point. In the Asian preaching pattern articulated by Kim, the theme merely helps to shape the spiral in its descent.

Holistic Knowing

Holistic knowing involves a balance between intellectual study and intuitive meditation. Kim explains that "human consciousness is not separated into compartments or stages," but that study and meditation combine to nurture an intuition that can be grasped collectively. "In Asian communication," she writes, "intuition is not simply one aspect of human consciousness that assists in achieving an emotional climax or intellectual understanding but is a contributor to a condition of unity in which all perceptive faculties generate a spontaneous grasp of truth."[37] Holistic knowing is key to the highest goal of human life, which is the fulfillment of the self through the cultivation of the humanity of others. This is a central principle of Confucianism. Here self and community are inseparable and the well-being of one is tied to the other. Similar insights have been noted in the discipline of classical western rhetoric, which draws not just from logic (*logos*) but from emotion (*pathos*), and the character of the people, shaping ethical action (*ethos*).[38]

The Pursuit of Consensus

The emphasis on consensus works in conjunction with holistic knowing. Individual opinion is secondary to that of the community in pursuit of consensus. This aspect of Asian preaching is in stark contrast to the western rhetorical tradition in which the preacher's job is to persuade through argumentation, establishing a certain opinion or a clear view, which holds sway over others. This is the basic assumption of deductive patterns of preaching. The Asian pattern that seeks consensus has more in common with an inductive style whose goal is to invite the congregation to discover and arrive at their own conclusion. A direct instructional style of communication is discouraged.

The Dialogues of Silence

Silence is not an absence of sound in preaching. It is a mode of dialogue, integral to the Asian sermonic pattern that Kim outlines. The beginning step in creating a sermon includes meditating on the text. This requires silence. Kim cites a very well-known wisdom in Korea that is also found in Japan, concerning the nature of the communication between lovers.[39] The example is of a young couple who sit together in silence gazing at the moon. When the young man simply observes, "How beautiful is the moon," the young woman understands from the context and the silence preceding the utterance that the young man is proposing. The point being made here is that a lot can be communicated in silence and indirect speech. To get a message across, long moments of silence and indirect communication can be very effective.

There is a saying that "listening is the beginning, silence is the hearing."[40] Making room for silence in the sermon is important to allow the listeners a chance to absorb what is being said.[41] Silence and sound, two opposite poles, exist interdependently. Sound cannot communicate without silence. Musicians know this truth. Music, making sound, is impossible without silences to resonate, bounce back, and absorb the notes.[42]

Indirect Communication

Normally in Western culture, good communication means that speakers come to a point directly, clearly, and right away, if possible. That is why a propositional, expository, and deductive pattern of preaching discussed earlier has a long-standing record and continues to occupy a dominant place in homiletics. Preachers using this pattern benefit from using it when the message needs to be proclaimed directly and clearly. It is a virtue and a gift to be able to get the message across in this way. The so-called bread-and-butter sermon of the church has flourished for these reasons.[43] But in Asian culture, particularly in Japan, as Kim points out, there can be more virtue to an indirect message. Listeners in such Asian contexts expect a message to take a long time to arrive. In some cases, it is even acceptable if the message does not fully arrive. It is simply open-ended or preaching to be continued. This can be illustrated using the language structure of Korean and Japanese. Kim points out that "while English has a predicate verb right after the subject noun or pronoun, Korean and Japanese place the verb at the end of the sentence."[44] Thus, the speaker or the hearer in communication must be patient, waiting to listen to the end of the sentence to get its meaning.

One of the positive implications of indirect communication for preaching is that it helps us appreciate intuition, evokes our imagination, builds suspense, and encourages the listener to tap into unknown possibilities. Sondra Willobee suggests that making hearers wait to get an answer to a question serves as an effective preaching hook.[45] Indirect communication reaches beyond cognitive areas of the brain and is conducive to holistic knowing.

AFRICAN AMERICAN PATTERNS

At the outset, we suggest that there is more than one African American pattern. Preaching scholar Cleophus J. LaRue has shown how diverse African American preaching patterns are.[46] African American preachers have drawn from their African oral traditions and ancestral wisdoms and incorporated these into the current preaching context in various ways. This section seeks only to highlight a central feature that seems to be prevalent in traditional African American preaching.

African American preaching patterns take emotional experiences seriously. African American homiletician Henry Mitchell suggests that the emotional impact of a sermon is connected to the need to instill resiliency in people in the face of injustice and suffering. It is imperative to make these experiences visible, naming them clearly and candidly. LaRue describes the African American preaching patterns as follows: "start slow, rise high, strike fire, sit down in a storm."[47] His description suggests that an African American preaching pattern can be understood as celebratory enthusiasm building to a climax. An essential aspect of this sermon pattern is the antiphonal call-and-response as preacher and congregation vocally and emotionally engage in the preaching event.[48] In this case, the main message is toward the end and is introduced for maximum emotional effect. It should be noted here that often a deductive statement is conveyed in the introduction and sermon title but the celebration at the end is not always tied to the sermon's message since it often is about atonement and repentance.

African American preaching patterns are similar to and different from feminist and Asian preaching patterns as both value emotion and intuition as well as experiences. The "deep feelings" or "godly emotions"[49] of the African American approach, however, involves explicit vocalization, while Asian preaching normally relies on silence and indirect expression. Both patterns of preaching styles and homiletic movements claim that Christian faith is not born "of" rational argument but of many experiences including emotional and intuitive ones.[50] A good postcolonial preacher will engage all these sources of faith.

HISPANIC AND LATINX PREACHING PATTERNS

Emerging patterns from Hispanic and Latinx preaching highlight their cross-cultural and bilingual contexts. According to Kenneth Davis, preachers addressing Latinx congregations can assume that their audience is not homogenous. Inevitably the assembly consists of "first and second-generation families who vary in their mastery of Spanish, differ by accent, and come from distinct Hispanic countries."[51] Davis observes that this peculiar reality must be taken seriously by the preacher. These cross-cultural, intergenerational, and bilingual realities are a distinctive characteristic of the Latinx preaching context. Generally, however, these diverse identities are unified by a common experience of migration and displacement. The sermon pattern necessarily addresses this experience of social dislocation in a way that binds the assembly together despite their differences.

These differences that Pablo Jiménez and Justo González raise another unique identity for Latinx community helpfully articulated by Virgilio Elizondo as *mestizo*, descendants of a Spaniard and an Indigenous person and *mulato* as the offspring of an African and a Spaniard. These mixed and hybridized experiences are important markers to both name as a brutal violence of European colonial conquest and its legacy and lift up the assembly's resilience and resistance as an essential part of a sermon pattern in Latinx diverse communities.[52]

Jiménez claims that in Latinx sermons, there are unique points of contact between the social location of the Latinx people and the biblical narrative.[53] This includes a critical analysis of the postcolonial reality combined with the hermeneutical reflection of the text but does not neglect emotive cultural elements either. Latinx preaching draws attention to Latinx narratives found in contemporary and ancient texts (poetry, song, plays, stories, proverbs, testimonies), including *corridos* (folk ballads) and *alabados* (song).[54] This pattern makes use of examples from ordinary lives and provides a powerful witness to the resilience of Latinx lives.[55]

A POSTCOLONIAL PATTERN OF PREACHING

A postcolonial preaching pattern is built on previous patterns, noting that all the different patterns I have explored in this chapter are important. This claim may not be a surprise because postcolonial work focuses on reconstruction. By reconstruction, I mean the work that involves both deconstruction of a problematic tradition with scrutiny, and the reconstruction of a new tradition with imagination. It is having a bifocal vision, having Yin and Yang eyes, as raised in chapter 2. It is about being able to see the dead (tradition, though there is much within tradition that is not dead, and stories from the past) and the living (context and the current reality) in order to shape the future. We will revisit this vision as a way of interpreting the Bible in chapter 6 when we discuss Exegesis. To underscore the work of reconstruction also means that searching for a postcolonial pattern of preaching debunks binary constructions and denounces cultural essentialism and ideologies that privilege the status quo. A postcolonial pattern equips preachers and people involved in preaching to negotiate complex realities, traverse various terrains, and deliver invigorating messages of hope and justice. Thus, it would be useful to capture findings from the previous patterns in order to show how they are conducive to a pattern of postcolonial preaching.

SERMON EXAMPLE

The following sermon happens to be an essentially inductive pattern that draws on several elements of the socially located patterns discussed earlier. Among these is an attention to a holistic message that incorporates the rhythms of life with highlights of self-disclosure (feminist). The sermon spirals down under the gravity of the theme of spiritual community, building emotionally to a question about how the dead, by lifting up a cultural practice, may continue to be an important part of our families who need care and attention (Asian). Finally, the sermon takes for granted a hybrid community of different ages and cultural backgrounds (African and Latinx). In this way, it is a sermon that uses a postcolonial pattern in its creation.

"Together for Better"

Lev. 23:15–16; John 4:5–15

Members of the family are busy cooking food and making cake from the first rice harvest of the year. The aroma of the sesame seeds and sesame oil in the sticky rice cake called *Songpyun* fill the whole house making mouths water. Fresh vegetables and fruits from the field are being prepared. It is the morning of the harvest moon festival in Korea. Children and adults put on new clothes.

A table is set. Special dishes that dearly departed family members loved are placed on a low table in front of a photo of them. Members of the family bow to the table. Someone (usually the father of the household) puts chopsticks on the bowl containing the favorite dish of the dearly departed. The living feed the dead. All stop and pause. The living and dead converse in silence and in spirit. Then the family bows once again, prostrating themselves, face flat on the ground, paying reverence, and expressing their gratitude. When everything is done, the family eats together.

This ceremony, which I have just described to you, called *Jesa* has been observed in East Asia and around the world for the two and a half millennia since the followers of Confucius began it. They did so in order to instill a sense of filial loyalty among the members of the family, a central pillar of Confucian ethics.

On the last weekend, people celebrated *choosuk*, or *hangawi* as it is often called in Korea, the Mid-autumn Harvest Festival. *Hangawi* is a celebration on the fifteenth day of the eighth month of the Lunar Calendar, one of the biggest festivals in the Korean calendar. It is a celebration like Christmas. I always feel excited when the time comes around. I cannot pass up this chance to share this part of my culture with you today, the first chapel after *hangawi*, as we celebrate the beginning of the 2019 school year and a harvest of learners.

The Korean thanksgiving celebration *hangawi* has parallels in the Bible. The feast of Weeks that together we heard read from the book of Leviticus was a harvest festival, though it usually fell between late April and June, depending on the location in Israel. It is called the Feast of Harvest in Exod. 23:16 and the First Fruits of the Wheat Harvest in Exod. 34:22. It is a festival of rejoicing over the abundant gifts of food that God has given in the harvest.

Korean ancestors who were farmers thought that the full moon in August was the biggest and the brightest. They needed it to be big and bright because it was a time when they might need to work late to get the harvest in. Just as Saskatchewan farmers are out in their combines today, some of them working around the clock by the lights of their machines to get the grain cut at exactly the right time.

So too did Korean farmers work late into the evening to get the rice and other grain in to maximize its quality and quantity. For this reason, they might have appreciated the glorious and generous light of the moon shining on them.

When the first harvest was collected, when their hard labor had been blessed by the shining full moon, what did people of Korea and people of Israel do? They gathered! They gathered and gave thanks to God the creator. The spirit of the Korean harvest celebration and the Jewish feast of weeks' celebration guide us into meditation on the importance of gathering.

We are gathered here at the chapel; Why? Because it is Wednesday 1:30 pm? Do we gather because the bell has rung? Yes! But, of course, it is more than that. More mysterious. Something out of the ordinary calls us to gather. Something causes us to pause from our business of learning and teaching. Gathered as a worshipping community, we are brought into each other's presence and God's presence. In this regular practice of gathering, our souls are fed, our spirits are watered, our bodies are cared for, and our whole selves are changed.

A similar, yet different mysterious encounter, a subtle, yet powerful guiding hand enabled a gathering under a shining bright sun at noon time, near the well of our ancestor Jacob. It was an encounter between two people, which was only recorded by the Gospel of John. The ancient well at the edge of the Samaritan town was a natural place to gather. It was nothing extraordinary.

On the other hand, this encounter was not ordinary at all; certainly not conventional. High noon was a strange time for a woman to draw water. Usually people waited until the heat of the day had worn off before they came to get water. Not so for the Samaritan woman in this story. And Jesus was not supposed to converse with the woman from Samaria. Jews were not supposed to ask for water from gentiles.

Nevertheless, there they were. Together. Each drawn by a need; a thirst for water, yes, but for something deeper than that. Drawn like the water into the cupped hands of the Creator, two people, alienated from each other and their communities, gathered in that place.

Jesus, the respected Jewish rabbi, asked for a drink, showing his weakness. This woman from Samaria, vulnerable as a woman with complicated life experiences, boldly engages him in conversation, challenging his authority with hers. Both are vulnerable; both are needy.

In providing the necessities of life to one another, both are nurtured and transformed. The woman from Samaria, who has been judged and cast out from her community because of her storied past, was changed by this gathering. Jesus, a wandering Jewish teacher, thirsty for kindness, was also changed as his calling was affirmed by the woman and those whom she later brought to meet him.

We, at Emmanuel College, seek such encounters. We, at Emmanuel, yearn for such affirmation too, as we discern and fulfill our vocation and our purpose of life in ministry and beyond.

Ministry is not an easy calling. Proclaiming the good news today requires patience and perseverance. Let's be honest. Sometimes we must face tough questions. One of the questions that still haunts those who serve the church today is the question of heaven and hell. Is there heaven? Is there hell? And if so, who is going where? It is a tricky question to answer.

Some people will want us to confirm for them their belief in a spiritual geography with two places, one in the clouds and one in the fiery depths of the earth. Others will want us to deny it but in our denial of an ancient tradition, expect that it calls into question all of our most cherished beliefs. Perhaps the following will provide us with a possible approach.

Let's imagine two human conditions. We'll call one heaven. The other we'll say is hell. Let us say that in both conditions, hungry people are placed in front of a table full of the most delicious food. And they are given chopsticks!

But these are not ordinary chopsticks. These chopsticks are longer than our arm's length. It is therefore impossible to feed oneself with them. In heaven and hell, people are not allowed to eat unless they use these chopsticks. (It is unfair for those who are used to eating with only forks, isn't it?) So in this situation what is the difference between heaven and hell?

The answer is that in heaven people use their chopsticks to feed one another. The only way you do not get hungry is to feed others rather than trying to feed yourself and to accept food from others who are offering it to you. The hungry are fed at the mercy of and by the grace of others. People in hell don't know the simple yet profound truth that in order to be fed we must feed others.

Are we taking the time to feed and be fed in this capitalistic world? Are we neglecting the celebration of abundance to which we are all called by God's grace? Economic and ecological injustices emerge consequently from the life of hell we chose to lead. People all over the world are hungering and thirsting. And if they cannot eat, if they cannot drink, if we cannot feed them, neither can we be fed.

There are frightening forces at work in our world and within us that are killing us, tearing us apart. We see the walls going up to keep people separated from one another, the barriers erected that allow some to hoard wealth and food in one place and keep it from people in another. We hear the hateful words that float in the streets and in our homes, that travel over the Internet, dividing people into categories of race, gender, sexual orientation, religion, and social class, pronouncing some worthy of respect and others worthy of disdain.

We sense the forces of history like colonization that has robbed some of land and language and invisibly enforces the identities of haves and have-nots. We utter the message blatantly or we whisper to one another and to ourselves, justifying the violence against others, against ourselves, and against God.

Amid such subtle, yet, all pervasive and inherently death-dealing forces of evil, the Gospel story of the encounter between Jesus and the Samaritan woman draw us together. This encounter offers water that is eternal freeing our substances to flow along the same course. This encounter invites us to be bold, encouraging us to learn to use chopsticks to feed the other, practicing the act of receiving. It shows how to rehearse the life of heaven, the realm of God here and now in this place and in this particularly challenging time.

How many of you have gone on canoe trips?

Some of you must be good paddlers, and some of you, like me, are beginners. On my first canoe trip, my son, Noah had just turned two, and I was seven months pregnant with my daughter Hannah. My father-in-law was a keen paddler and always pushed for these trips. My in-laws were all good paddlers, too. The same could not be said of me! And of course, Noah was too small to paddle. He was a toddler. When we portaged, Noah was carried by one of the family. On the lake, while others paddled hard, all I could do was to sit in the bottom of the canoe and be paddled along. Noah and I were kind of luggage, dead weight, unable to help the seasoned canoers.

I am sure that some of my family felt anxious and stressed: Are we going to make it to the campsite before dark? The wind was blowing hard. The lake looked so big. Maybe the family felt like running (or swimming) away from me and Noah who were burden to them in a difficult situation. Yes, they felt stuck. Yet, they could not leave us and go ahead alone. They had to gently (but persistently) lead Noah and I, guide us, encourage us, and carry us. But at the campsite, I was on firmer ground, so to speak. I was able to help with the food. I was very happy to discover that my Canadian family enjoyed the rice that I cooked, and the kimchi, which I had brought.

A canoe trip drew the three generations and different cultures of our family together. This gathering, feeding, and carrying warmed our bodies and touched our souls. This experience taught a profound lesson of the interdependence of life, the key ingredient of the heavenly feast.

Next time when we take a family canoe trip, it will be different. My father-in-law passed away recently. It will be our first trip without him. I wonder, as we paddle across the lake, when we meet a strong wind or struggle along a portage, will he be in some sense, traveling with us? Will he be part of our company? Will he be enjoying the kimchi and rice we share together? Is his spirit also something we need to take care to include, to feed, and to care for? Would he also be supporting us in ways we were not aware of before?

Our academic community is much more powerful than we often realize when we stick together. Our community is much bigger than we realize when we include even those who have gone before us. Here is the Good News!

God is God, not of the dead, but of the living. Yet, the dead and the living are not separated but connected. Jesus and the Samaritan woman gathered at the well of Jacob, their ancestor. Jacob, Rachel and Leah, and Bilhah and Zilpah were surely there with them. We are gathered in this place, Emmanuel College, in the presence of the angels of God, as clouds of witnesses. They watch over us as we struggle through our difficult academic journey together. And we join with them in celebrating and in partaking in the food, feeding each other, carrying each other's pack, paddling together, embodying God's love for one another.

NOTES

1. HyeRan Kim-Cragg and EunYoung Choi, *The Encounters: Retelling the Bible from Migration and Intercultural Perspectives* (Daejeon: Daejanggan, 2013), 127–137.

2. While I use the term "pattern" to fit the syllable "P" of RIPPLE, other terms as forms, shapes, movements, structures, and designs will be used interchangeably.

3. H. Grady Davis, *Design for Preaching* (Minneapolis: Fortress, 1958), 1.

4. Ibid., 15.

5. Kim-Cragg, *Interdependence*, 135.

6. Paul Scott Wilson, *The Practice of Preaching* (Toronto: United Church Publishing House, 1996), 204.

7. Dave L. Bland, "Deductive," in *New Interpreter's Handbook of Preaching*, ed. Paul Scott Wilson (Nashville: Abingdon, 2008), 375.

8. Sallie McFague, "An Earthly Theological Agenda," in *Ecofeminism and the Sacred*, ed. Carol Adams (New York: Continuum, 1993), 96.

9. Otto Dieter, "Arbor Picta: The Medieval Tree of Preaching," *Quarterly Journal of Speech* 51 (1965): 123–144.

10. Bland, "Deductive," 376.

11. O. C. Edwards Jr., "Puritan Plain Style," in *New Interpreter's Handbook of Preaching*, ed. Paul Scott Wilson (Nashville: Abingdon, 2008), 411.

12. McClure, *Other-wise Preaching*, 67.

13. John McClure, "Expository Preaching," in *Concise Encyclopedia of Preaching*, ed. William Willimon and Richard Lischer (Louisville: Westminster John Knox, 1995), 131.

14. Allen, *Interpreting the Gospel*, 183.

15. Craddock, *As One without Authority*, 125.

16. Eugene L. Lowry, "The Revolution of Sermonic Shape," in *Listening to the Word: Studies in Honor of Fred. B. Craddock*, ed. Gail O's Day and Thomas Long (Nashville: Abingdon, 1993), 93–112.

17. Tom Long, "Forms," in *Concise Encyclopedia of Preaching*, ed. William H. Willimon and Richard Lischer (Louisville: Westminster John Knox, 1995), 148.

18. Eugene Lowry, *The Homiletical Plot: The Sermon as Narrative Art Form* (Louisville: Westminster John Knox, 2001), 26.

19. Charles Campbell, "Inductive Preaching," in *Concise Encyclopedia of Preaching*, ed. William H. Willimon and Richard Lischer (Louisville: Westminster John Knox, 1995), 271.

20. John C. Holbert, *Preaching Creation: The Environment and the Pulpit* (Eugene: Cascade, 2011), 85–87.

21. Ronald Allen, *I Will Tell You the Mystery: A Commentary on Preaching the Book of Revelation* (Eugene: Cascade, 2019), xvi–xix.

22. Paul Scott Wilson, "New Homiletic," in *New Interpreter's Handbook of Preaching*, ed. Paul Scott Wilson (Nashville: Abingdon, 2008), 400.

23. Christine Smith, "Feminist Preaching," in *Concise Encyclopedia of Preaching*, ed. William H. Willimon and Richard Lischer (Louisville: Westminster John Knox, 1995), 134.

24. John McClure, *Preaching Words: 144 Key Terms in Homiletics* (Louisville: Westminster John Knox, 2007), 35.

25. Smith, *Weaving the Sermon*, 140–150.

26. Shirley E. Held, *Weaving: A Handbook for Fiber Craftsmen* (New York: Hold, Rinehart & Winston, 1973).

27. Smith, *Weaving the Sermon*, 139.

28. Jana Childers and Clayton Schmit, eds., *Performance in Preaching: Bringing the Sermon to Life* (Grand Rapids: Baker, 2008).

29. Smith, *Weaving the Sermon*, 143.

30. Ibid., 146.

31. Mary Donovan Turner and Mary Lin Hudson, *Saved from Silence: Finding Women's Voice in Preaching* (St. Louis: Lucas Park, 2014), 100–115.

32. Smith, *Weaving the Sermon*, 146.

33. Held, *Weaving*, 314, cited in Ibid., 150.

34. Kim, *Preaching in the Presence of God*.

35. HyeRan Kim-Cragg, "Between and Beyond Asian-ness: A Voice of a Postcolonial Hybrid Korean-Canadian in the Diaspora," in *What Young Asian*

Theologians Are Thinking: The CSCA Christianity in Southeast Asia Series No 7, ed. Leow Theng Huat (Singapore: Trinity Theological College, 2014), 90–102.

36. Kim, *Preaching in the Presence of God*, 123.

37. Ibid. 115.

38. Jonathan Barnes, ed., "Rhetoric," in *The Complete Works of Aristotle* (Princeton: Princeton University Press, 1984), 2155.

39. John C. Condon and Fathi Yousef, *An Introduction to Intercultural Communication* (New York: Macmillan, 1987), 143, cited in Kim, *Preaching in the Presence of God*, 110.

40. Nelle Morton, *Journey Is Home* (Boston: Beacon, 1985), 87, cited in Turner and Hudson, *Saved from Silence*, 98.

41. Kim, *Preaching in the Presence of God*, 111.

42. HyeRan Kim-Cragg and Joanne Doi, "Intercultural Threads of Hybridity and Threshold Spaces of Learning," *Religious Education* 107:3 (2012): 262–275.

43. Wilson, *The Practice of Preaching*, 205.

44. Kim, *Preaching in the Presence of God*, 112.

45. Sondra Willobee, *The Write Stuff: Crafting Sermons that Captures and Convince* (Louisville: Westminster John Knox, 2009), 11–28.

46. LaRue, *The Heart of Black Preaching*, 68–113.

47. Ibid., 11.

48. Evans E. Crawford with Thomas H. Troeger, *The Hum: Call and Response in African American Preaching* (Nashville: Abingdon, 1995), 20.

49. Henry Mitchell, *Celebration and Experience in Preaching* (Nashville: Abingdon, 1991), 27–28.

50. Kim, *Preaching in the Presence of God*, 114.

51. Kenneth G. Davis, OFM CONV, "Cross-Cultural Preaching," in *Preaching and Culture in Latino Congregations*, 42.

52. Virgilio Elizondo, *Galilean Journey* (Maryknoll: Orbis, 1983) and *The Future Is Mestizo: Life Where Cultures Meet*, revised edition (Boulder: University Press of Colorado, 2000).

53. Pablo Jiménez, "In Search of a Hispanic Model of Biblical Interpretation," *Journal of Hispanic/ Latino Theology* 3:2 (November 1995): 44–64.

54. Davis, "Cross-Cultural Preaching," 54.

55. Justo González, "By the River of Babylon," in *Preaching Justice: Ethnic and Cultural Perspectives*, ed. Christine Smith (Cleveland: United Church Press, 1998), 80–97.

Chapter 5

Language

Becoming a Postcolonial Polyglot with Cultural Linguistic Competency

Now the whole earth had one language and the same words. . . . And the Lord said, "Look, they are one people, and they have all one language; and this is only the beginning of what they will do; nothing that they propose to do will now be impossible for them. Come, let us go down, and confuse their language there, so that they will not understand one another's speech. . . . Therefore it was called Babel, because there the Lord confused the language of all the earth; and from there the Lord scattered them abroad over the face of all the earth."

—Gen. 11:1, 6–7, 9

Continuing to integrate previous chapters, we will explore preaching language as something more than the language of speech or writing, but in a range of diverse manifestations. A postcolonial approach to preaching is aware of many different ways we communicate. In the same ways that pattern communicate meaning, alongside the messages for which they are a vehicle, the language we choose communicates a meaning on its own. The words we choose and the context in which we place them may suggest a meaning contradictory to the message we hope to communicate. For example, a preacher that wishes to emphasize the need for reconciliation between indigenous people and settler populations may speak of "Canada's native people," implying the state's paternal oversight in a way that contradicts the stated goal of the sermon. Likewise, the use of the body or neglect of the body for communicating can also send an unintended message. Also, the courage of a preacher to engage with language traditions outside of the ones they are most familiar with can send an important signal to the congregation about the kind of vision for the community the preacher has in mind. All these aspects of language will be explored in this chapter. R. S. Sugirtharajah, a pioneer in postcolonial biblical criticism and an advocate of the use of vernacular languages in interpreting the text, underscores its importance: "Colonialism is not simply a system of economic and military control, but a systematic cultural penetration and domination." Thus, he argues that postcolonial preaching seeks to understand and use various modes of language to tackle the devastating legacy of "psychological, intellectual and cultural colonialization."[1]

PREACHING LANGUAGE AS THEOLOGICAL BODY LANGUAGE

Christians have described Jesus as the Word made flesh. Christian theology is incarnational. God's message is embodied in the acts of Jesus who surrendered his own life for the life of the world, whose risen body is still at work in the world and in our own bodies, the body of the church. Barbara Brown Taylor captures this point in this way, "Jesus speaks body language—physical, sensory language his hearers could see and hear and touch.... The Incarnate Word preached ... so that no one who stood in his presence could miss his point."[2] Preaching as theological body language uses the language of embodied experience. The language of human experience is "language steeped in the mystery of incarnation by which the shape of God is revealed in the world."[3] In this sense, we are called to preach the gospel "tangibly."[4] For Henry Mitchell, it is the familiarity of an experience shared in story that can embody a message. While the parable of Jesus as the lost sheep, for example, may not be familiar to contemporary ears, they were familiar to the audiences around Jesus.[5] People understood this parable because they knew the experience of being a shepherd. That is why good preaching is not to tell people what to believe but to help people connect their faith with their experiences. Through these familiar embodied experiences being shared in preaching, God is named and imagined. The effectiveness with which the preacher communicates in language, which the body understands, can be ascertained through the bodily response of the congregation. African American homiletician Teresa Fry Brown, building on Mitchell's work, underscores the many and complex factors, which help a congregation to receive a sermon as an embodied experience. She writes, "Listener acceptance or rejections of sermons often has more to do with the differences in ethnic, gender, or racial characteristics of the preacher and congregation." The acceptance of the sermon is communicated in body language, she continues, as people "wave a hand, clap, stand up, run, cry, shake their heads, rock back and forth, moan, hum, kneel, or even throw items at the preacher in an affirming sort of way."[6] The body language of the congregation is relational and responsive; it performs a kind of theological language in conversation with the preacher. Cleophus J. LaRue adds that "antiphonality, repetition, alliteration, syncopation, formulas, thematic imagery, voice merging, and sacred time . . . can evoke a sense of God's awe and mystery in the listening congregation."[7] Because body language is relational, it enables the congregation, preacher, and God to be in conversation.

The development of the language of the body in concert with the language of the mind is essential for effective postcolonial preaching. Richard Ward stresses the importance of performing the text for preachers and congregants as they try to grasp its meaning. Ward argues, for example, that the physical act of simply reading a scripture passage can make a difference to how it is understood in comparison to a silent private reading. This difference is amplified when a text is performed or dramatized as performer and hearer are drawn into a more embodied experience. He shares his own experience when he knelt in performing the text of the woman who was bent over for eighteen years (Luke 13:11). Ward realized that he, as a white male able-bodied person of status, had never had to bow and kneel to anyone. The shock of recognition of his privilege happened because he used what he called the language of "body thinking."[8] There is a difference in exegetical impact when one performs the text. The appreciation of a "body thinking" practice enables preachers to find their own voice (a voice of privilege or of vulnerability, for example) and to discover God's voice in community and with his/her/their own body. Here the use of the body as language points to the importance of the medium, which calls to mind the well-known phrase of Marshall McLuhan "the medium is the message." The embodiment, the tone of the voice, mannerisms, pauses and the gestures of the preacher's body language matter as much as the content of the message.

Bodies communicate things in ways preachers do not always feel comfortable with. The fact that the preacher's body can communicate things the preacher does not mean or want to share makes a preacher feel vulnerable. Which preacher wants to look nervous in front of a congregation, or lose control of their emotions? Anyone who has experienced public speaking will be able to relate to this fear. Research shows that a very common fear is the fear of public speaking. Studies suggest that the fear of public speaking even surpasses the fear of death![9] This fact should engender a healthy respect for our bodies in the act of preaching. Bodies play an important role and carry a message. Our words and our bodies must act together to effectively deliver a sermon. Therefore, preachers should get in touch with their bodies in the process of preparing to preach, and congregations should be invited to exercise their own bodies in the course of the worship event as a way of harnessing the communicative power of the incarnate Word.

Preaching that focuses on spoken language alone runs the risk of overlooking those who cannot hear. How the absence of sign language interpreters in most Sunday worship services excludes members of the deaf community is something that churches need to consider. When biblical scholars and homileticians assume spoken language as the language of the Bible and that of the pulpit they unduly privilege the hearing community and marginalize those who cannot hear. Kathy Black points out that the common biblical notion that not being able to hear is a sign of not having faith is potentially harmful to the deaf community. She cites Fred Craddock, who wrote "the event of the Word of God needs the ear, for faith comes by hearing" and David Buttrick, who also connects faith with hearing when he states: "'faith comes by hearing,' if that is the case, we strive to be heard." Likewise, she continues, Walter Brueggemann writes, "it is speech and only speech that bonds God and human creatures."[10] The prevalence of this metaphor is keeping us from appreciating other ways, figurative and literal, that the message can be delivered and received.

We conclude the discussion of the embodied nature of preaching language with a note about the body extending beyond our individual physical selves. As alluded above, just as preaching should not be understood exclusively in terms of a verbal exercise, neither should it be understood as a solo endeavor. An appreciation of the role of the preacher as shared and owned by the whole community is essential. Preaching has no weight unless it is the corporate body of faith that lives by it. Christian preaching seeks a world that is shaped by the gospel. It is to rehearse the reign of God together.[11] Preaching as a theological body language uses the language of social relationships that is formed by the community. Even more radically, the preaching act should be seen as involving all of creation. St. Francis, the medieval saint, was well known for his practice of preaching to birds and animals, the trees, and the stars. In the same way, the experience of receiving a divine message in the song of a bird, the sight of a flowing river, the feel of the wind, is quite common. Jesus, himself, spoke of these experiences. This communal dimension of homiletic language underscores the power of the gospel that is transmitted in the use of the language of the stories we tell, the responses we illicit, the signs we perform, and the meanings we receive from the human and nonhuman community surrounding us.

PREACHING LANGUAGE AS INCLUSIVE LANGUAGE

Preaching language is a marker of inclusivity. It can affirm a group in positive terms or label them in negative ways. Language that reinforces a power imbalance within the community should be guarded against. One example that is often pointed to is the language that describes the colors black and white in judgment-laden ways: it is detrimental for black to be constantly associated with being dangerous and dirty and white to be associated with purity and goodness. These subtle and not-so-subtle associations are often connected to discourse about race in society today. What is more is that they are powered by long traditions in the English language and interpretations of biblical stories. Ossie Davis as actor, playwright, and director wrote that "the English language is my enemy." This assertion was born out of the context in which there are 134 common synonyms for the word "white" in the English language, but there are only 10 that are slightly negative. These words include "whitewash," "gray," and "pale." By contrast, for the word "black" there are 120 synonyms, none of which are positive, and 60 synonyms are very negative connoting threat, evil, and wickedness such as "black market" and "black mail."[12]

This disturbing aspect of the English language has infiltrated stories from the Bible. Take the word "Ham" from the Hebrew Bible as an example. The story of Noah in Genesis (9:18–27) is an important text to highlight because it has been used to justify slavery of black people. An interpretation of this text identifies Ham as the progenitor of those with black skin because Noah had cursed him. Thus, he is said to be the ancestor of Africans traced back to Canaan. David M. Goldenberg has investigated every reference to blacks in Jewish literature back to the seventh century and discovered a misreading of Hebrew and other Semitic languages that led to the translation of the word "Ham" as "dark, black or heat." But he also argues that there was no anti-black sentiment in ancient Greece, Rome, or Arabia.[13] It was the colonial world in particular that most twisted the Ham story in Genesis and used it to justify the enslavement of black people in the modern era. The transatlantic slave trade that began in the sixteenth century was born of the colonial period, and is mainly responsible for the fact that by the nineteenth century, proslavery Americans were drawn to the story of Ham because it helped endorse this politically sanctioned practice.[14]

In the same way sexist language is also lethal and embedded deeply within English and the biblical languages. Not only are men represented as the norm, but also male designations such as master and bachelor have positive connotations compared to labels of women such as mistress and spinster. Stories in the Bible, such as the story of Adam and Eve in Genesis, have been used to reinforce these attitudes. Recent scholarship has begun to push back against traditions that denigrate women, however. For example, the interpretation of Adam as connotative of male gender has been contested. The Hebrew word *adam* from *adama* can indeed mean a male and even be the proper name Adam, but it can also be a generic term for a mortal, or a human being. On the contrary, the counterpart of Adam, Eve, representing women, has been narrowly defined as "helper" to downgrade her role as subordinate and inferior to men. Yet, we know that the creation of Eve, referring as the term *ezer ke-negdo*, in Gen. 2:18 is "an equal helper as his partner." Yet, the omission of "equal" as translated by the NRSV results in reinforcing sexist hierarchy and distorting further the meaning of the word, Eve, *chavah* in Hebrew as "the life giver."[15]

There are many other examples of the way our language traditions exclude and degrade people. The common reference to the Jewish Scriptures or Hebrew Bible as the Old Testament, for example, suggests a supersessionist bias and has contributed to anti-Semitic views.[16] Simple grammar can exhibit bias as well. Many of us have been taught to use a passive tense in English, while avoiding subjective "I" language when writing academic papers for the sake of ensuring neutral and objective inquiry. But we now know that seeking neutrality and objectivity masks the white Eurocentric hegemonic normativity at work. In the case of raising awareness of racism in preaching, Christine Smith points out that instead of saying "the railroad was built," preachers can say, "Chinese laborers built much of it, and were terribly oppressed in the process."[17] Otherwise the agent or the perpetrator is hidden so the contribution of the action is thereby diffused. Simple sentence structures such as "she is a Turk" rather than "she is Turkish" or "he is a Jew" compared to "he is Jewish" can evoke prejudice and social stereotypes and need to be guarded against.[18]

In the social realm beyond religious and Christian communities, we find the US designation of undocumented immigrants as resident aliens. This word "alien" conjures an image of a person, or even a space creature, who does not belong in a given place. The preacher must always be wary of the potential of language to imply exclusion or unwelcome to whole groups of people.

The inclusive nature of congregations depends, to a large extent, upon the language coming from the pulpit. The Bible offers us examples of radical inclusivity. The creation story in Genesis 1, for example, establishes the common origin of all human beings, as well as the connections that exists between humans and all creation. It helps to explain why the community must seek inclusion in all social relationships. The language of inclusivity resonates with the Hebrew word for justice, which means "putting relationships in their right order in the light of the covenant."[19] In this regard, preaching on just relationships is not an option, but an obligation.

Preaching language is never neutral. It discloses and masks power. Language carries bias in both positive and negative ways. Language as power acts on society to perpetuate certain ideologies, establishes structural relations, generates visions of the future, spreads fear and hatred, and attacks oppression. Because language is power, it must be situated in communities of accountability and structures of responsibility. Preaching language forms communities of faith. In this regard, preaching is the language of the church that is always reforming or in need of redemption. This is the heart of Protestant theology. Preaching language locates the Word within, rather than above, a community of faith. To use Kenneth Burke's theory of rhetoric, under normal circumstances, language reflects communicative properties within the community that authorizes and understands it.[20] That is why community and communication have the same etymology. Without the community of faith and its context, the language of preaching is not going to be communicated well. The message of Martin Luther King, Jr. is not going to be communicated accurately without the civil rights movements.

Reformed homiletician, Richard Lischer, articulates the language of preaching in relation to place: "Language is not neutral with regard to place. It is not transferable to other environments . . . . The specific context of sermons is the worship-scene in which the congregation gathers to remember, renew, and reportray its identity and mission."[21] Here he nuances the church as the preaching place of formation in terms of remembering, renewing, and reportraying the church's identity. He writes, "Preaching-as-formation is not content with its own eventfulness . . . . Preaching-as-formation explores the differences. In doing so, it becomes the voice of the church as a contrast-society."[22] Here the "voice" points to both the language of the church and the vocation of the church. The voice also indicates the collective and communal voice. Preaching cannot be represented by one person's persuasive address. It must involve the ceaseless activity of the church, open to critique and open to change (Acts 5:42). Inclusive language helps create the inclusive community. In turn, the inclusive community informs the inclusive language of the preacher.

PREACHING LANGUAGE AND CULTURE

I have earlier in the text explored the connection between the community and the message of a sermon. In this section, I will tease out the connection between language and culture. I contend that just as languages can both convey important meanings and problematic traditions, cultures can also be vehicles for meaning and sources of harmful attitudes and practices. The definition of language here has been expansive. But for the sake of limiting the scope of the issue to a discussion that fits within our parameters of a study of postcolonial preaching, I will limit our discussion of culture to the ways it permeates communal relationships affected by the colonial process. This narrow focus helps to pay close attention to the places where the preacher and the congregation do not share the same culture.

Preaching Language as a Cross-Cultural and Multilingual Exploration

Homileticians and theologians James Nieman and Thomas Rogers have examined the way that Anglo and non-Anglo cultures interact in the context of preaching. In their qualitative research on cross-cultural homiletics, interviewees who serve bilingual congregations were asked to share their experiences of navigating the limits of language in a context where a congregation has two distinct language backgrounds. They related the following observation from one of their interviews:

> A preacher in a Vietnamese church that operated *entirely in English* recalled his struggle with using the word *bread* in a sermon. The problem was not that the word failed to make sense, but that bread is used by Vietnamese as a frivolous pastry rather than a source of basic sustenance. Due to its oral orientation, this ethnic group heard "bread" concretely and so gave it a quite unintended meaning.[23]

Their research captured the challenge that English-speaking preachers have in navigating the complex nuances and layers of language. Yet, culture and language are so connected. Once understood, together, they can provide opportunities for learning on many different levels. This kind of an approach to language is essential in postcolonial preaching. But it requires a high degree of cultural literacy with an astute awareness of the dominance of Anglo culture in the North American context, which needs to be overcome. An important shift in the power dynamic takes place when people from cultures that are not dominant become teachers, and the people from white Anglo cultures become learners. In our diverse North American cultural settings where Anglo culture is still very dominant, a cross-cultural exchange can empower marginalized and minoritized cultures. An extensive examination and exploration of cultural wisdom as part of a study of the language of preaching, therefore, has the potential to contribute to the creation of more just relationships and empower resistance to the legacy of colonialism.

Faithful engagement with non-European cultures can provide many tools for reframing and decentering dominant North American culture. To illustrate this point, let us examine the East Asian ideogram for peace. Peace, *shalom* in Hebrew, is one of the core biblical and theological concepts inherited from our ancestors in faith. Korean, Japanese, Chinese, and many people from East Asian regions all express a concept of peace signified by the character, 和平 (pronounced *hwa* 和 *pyeong* 平 in Korean). The ideogram 和 (hwa) is itself a combination of two ideograms 禾 ("mi" meaning rice) and 口 ("gu" meaning mouth). The character 和 (hwa) then signifies that rice is meeting the mouth of a person, or in other words someone is eating. The ideogram 平 (pyeong) means "level" or "equal." The inference of the combination of 和 (hwa) and 平 (pyeong) is therefore that if everyone has the same amount to eat, there is peace. The concept of peace, otherwise abstract, is depicted in East Asia ideograms in a way that captures a physical, tactile, and daily experience. Jesus often used basic food stuffs as props in his parables. Peace, portrayed as the practice of sharing food fairly, helps people of faith imagine justice and rehearse the peace of God's realm on earth here and now. This is an example of the ways non-Western linguistic traditions provide resources for preachers who wish to explore important biblical and theological concepts such as *shalom*, while at the same time enabling them to make connections between biblical traditions and different cultural traditions.

In terms of the language of preaching that beholds a communal vision, rather than promoting a notion of individual salvation, Matthew Kim provides an example of understanding "you" in English, which is used both as singular and plural pronouns. For many African, African American, Asian, Asian North Americans, or Hispanic Americans who belong to collective cultures, the family unit is more important than the individual. In these cultures, people use the language of "you" often speaking to the entire community and family, not just to the individual.[24] The Korean language *uri* meaning "we" or "our" further elaborates this point. In the grammatical sense, *uri* refers to the first-person plural pronoun. However, *uri* is also commonly used in place of the possessive pronoun "my." Here the pronoun 'I' is not singular but collective. What is particularly interesting about this word *uri* in Korean is that even when talking to someone who is clearly not related, Koreans still use this linguistic terminology as if they were. For example, people in Korea often introduce one's spouse, "This is our husband" or "This is our wife," even though "my husband/wife" is grammatically correct and this reference does not indicate that they are actually in polygamy relationships.[25]

Cultural Language as a Marker of Power Differentials

Culturally relevant examples embedded in language vary. Cultural idioms and sayings that permeate everyday life are important as preaching illustrations but some of them are also embedded with prejudice that helps to maintain a status quo benefiting one group over another. Cultural sayings or words, for example, sometimes reflect traditions steeped in patriarchy and contain sexist teachings. The following Korean proverb is a case in point: "When three women gather and talk, a dish may break." This proverb basically suggests that women's camaraderie is unwelcome and women's voices, especially collective voices, are dangerous and destructive. When such a proverb is used to illustrate a scriptural text such as 1 Cor. 14:34, "women should be silent in church," the impact is to reinforce a negative interpretation and communicate a harmful message in preaching. The views of this proverb are embedded deeply in East Asian culture. The Chinese ideogram 姦, means sly, cunning, conceited, or unrighteous. It is composed of three 女s, an ideogram meaning woman. The suggestion, of course, is to associate a negative characteristic with a group of women. When using a culturally specific example, it is unfair and plainly dangerous to essentialize that culture. By using this example, I do not mean to suggest that patriarchy in Asia is any worse than it is in other parts of the world, North America for example. I use it here simply to point out that power differentials are embedded in language and culture and that we need to be conscious of this fact when we preach and use cultural illustrations and examples.

Culturally embedded power differentials are intersectional. Attention to the intersectionality enables an interrogation of cultural imperialism and colonialism in addition to other oppressions (racism, classism, sexism, and ableism) so that preaching can be truly liberative. Just as anthropologists in the past century have been implicated in "the ongoing subjugation of some people as inferior while valorizing others as superior," preachers are in danger of contributing to the problem if they are not careful.[26] One way to undress this cultural subjugation through preaching language is, as Christine Smith asserts, to work to make the power differentials explicit when we compose sentences. As an example, she juxtaposes these two sentences: "the white captor raped an African woman held in captivity" versus "the master raped his slave."[27] In the first, the injustice is more fully revealed while in the second, the injustice seems almost taken for granted. This example speaks to the intersectionality of race, slavery, and patriarchy.

The intersecting issues of social inequality and oppression found in the examples often come to the fore in communities when different ethnic and racial differences come together. It is imperative then, for preachers in a postcolonial context to prepare themselves to deal with such inequalities. Matthew Kim writes, "Preachers are students of cultures—biblical cultures as well as contemporary ones. Perhaps more than ever, ethnicity and cultural differences have wedged themselves into the homiletical equation, so that preachers need to especially consider those listeners who diverge ethnically and culturally from themselves."[28] Elsewhere, Kim argues that the lack of attention to ethnicity is "a blind spot in homiletics."[29] An awareness of how language can be a carrier of systematic and structural power differentials, including those exacerbated by the history of colonialism, is essential in this regard.

The Linguistic Meaning of Culture and the History of Colonization

The notion and the meaning of culture have been important in the discussion of the language of preaching. But as a word in our language itself, culture requires some critical examination in the history of colonization. One meaning associated with the concept of culture came to the fore during the period of colonization. Certain colonial views of culture were strong well into the twentieth century. British colonialist Lord Lugard, for example, had the following to say in 1922:

> As Roman imperialism laid the foundations of modern civilisation, and led the wild barbarians of these islands along the path of progress, so in Africa today we are . . . bringing to the dark place of the earth, the torch of culture and progress, while ministering to the material needs of our own civilization . . . . We hold these countries because it is the genius of our race to colonise, to trade, and to govern.[30]

But does culture go hand in hand with progress? Is European culture identical to civilization? Is culture antithesis to nature?

Postcolonial scholar Robert Young has uncovered some of the colonial assumptions embedded with the word "culture" itself.[31] The English word "culture" comes from the Latin words *cultura* and *colere*. In English, these Latin words form the root of concepts associated with farming and settlement, such as cultivate and colonize. We can see here the connections of the word "culture" to the very process of colonization, a process that in settler colonies involved the occupation and cultivation of the land for farming.

Before the sixteenth century, the meaning of "culture" in English was associated with the physicality of the territory, the ploughing of the earth, and the cultivation of crops and animals. That is how the term "agriculture" was created, combing the word "Agri," from "Agro," meaning "a field" with the word "culture." Agriculture literally means "cultivate a field." Agriculture in English reflects an economic system based on farming.[32] Agriculture was seen as a way to supplant a nomadic hunting life and began to be described as a form of progress, as the advancement of human development in the period of the Enlightenment.

By the eighteenth century, the word "culture" was becoming closely associated with civilization and its intellectual trappings. It was also closely associated with the project of national education as a process of enhancing the human mind.[33] At the same time, this word began to be associated more closely with urban life.[34] Urban cultures were regarded as superior to the rural ones. Class and culture became associated with one another. Culture was also paired with the pseudoscientific concept of race. Class and race were constructed to promote a hierarchical imperial culture. Into this mix, the highly problematic ideology known as social Darwinism was added. It promoted, on the pretense of an objective scientific theory, the idea that some cultures were innately superior to others; and that superior cultures were destined to dominate, while inferior cultures were destined to be subjugated and disappear.[35]

In the case of Canada, the government of British North America promoted the migration of its citizens to occupy the land for the British crown. Cultivation of the soil by the colonists served to justify the British claim to the territory.[36] When Canada became an independent country in 1867, the new government laid claim to a vast territory north and west of the Great Lakes and doubled down on efforts to bring migrants to settle the territory. Many British citizens and others from all over Europe were hungry and poor and were strongly encouraged to emigrate to Canada where they were promised "free" land if they would "improve" it for agriculture. This process involved the signing of treaties with indigenous communities that were never honored by the Canadian government. At this time, compulsory national education was being introduced throughout the British Empire. The association of culture and civilization with this educational program compelled the Canadian government to create schools for indigenous children, which would work to supplant their "inferior" indigenous culture with a "superior" and "civilized" Canadian one. This is the origin of residential schools, a colonial legacy that has left a deep scar on Canadian society. The process outlined earlier makes a clear connection between the idea of culture and the process of colonialism.

In conclusion, postcolonial preachers need to be extra-conscious of using language as they consider its multilayered complexity in relation to body, inclusivity, culture, and colonialism. Attention to language in this regard has four significant implications for preaching.

First, preaching as body language needs to be understood broadly. A broad view of preaching as body language appreciates that homiletical language is performative and seeks "faithfulness not only to the message of a text, but to its purpose expressed through its performative language."[37] The language of preaching as body language yields not only biblically sound and theologically apt. Good sermons having body language also make an experientially abundant impact. Here, appreciation of the life experiences of the people in the congregation leads to an appreciation of the church as a corporate body where diversity, differences, and plurality of experiences are shared, negotiated, and renewed. Body language as a church's language of preaching is learning a new communal language together, making sure that an individual or a particular group cannot dominate. Preaching inclusive language seeks just relationships, captured in the kin-dom of God, as discussed in chapter 1.

Secondly, the attention to the relational body language of the congregation also points to the inclusivity of language and highlights the importance of listening, speaking, and other ways of communication. If one of the goals of preaching is to form an inclusive congregation, attention to the subtle and not-so-subtle ways language can be exclusive is of utmost importance. So too, are the ways a healthy inclusive community helps to shape language in healthy inclusive ways.

Thirdly, the language of preaching needs to be sensitive to cultural differences and use those differences to its advantage. We highlighted ways that the intersection of language can illuminate the meaning of a biblical concept. We also discussed how the use of other languages decenters the dominant culture and language, English in most North American contexts, and provides others from nondominant cultural ways to participate in the act of preaching and the life of the church in new ways.

Finally, the language of preaching needs to wrestle with the cultural baggage of colonialism. It is abundantly clear that culture as a social construction has been imbricated with the idea of European civilization. Western cultural supremacy and civilization have been preached and used in evangelization, conversion, and the proselytization process. Even the concept of culture is laden with colonial baggage. One way to explore this inter-relatedness of colonial language in preaching is to contest the problem of anthropocentrism, as well as cultural, racial, and religious hierarchy as lingering colonial problems we face today.

SERMON EXAMPLE

The following sermon was preached in a service to mark Asian Heritage Month, May 2020. I was asked to teach something about Asian culture as a guest preacher at a congregation in Toronto. I took the liberty of giving a lesson on the Korean and Chinese language as well as an indigenous language that has embedded in a profound wisdom about family, which is connected to individual and communal well-being. The sermon provides information on the meaning of the biblical Greek word, *Paraclet*, conjuring up the image of the protector who is like an intimate friend helping and comforting the ones who are in distress. The keyword "family" is captured in the language of Jesus who also uses a family term, "orphan," in teaching his disciples about God's desire for our well-being.

"A Bound Family Vine"

Ps. 66: 13–15 John 14:15–21

I feel blessed to join you today to celebrate Asian heritage Month. I feel sorry not being able to see you in person but excited about a new way of worshipping via Zoom.

Asia is big. Asia is 45 million square kilometers, which is twice as big as North America. Asia is diverse. It is home to 4.5 billion people. Over 2,300 living languages are spoken there. Many religions are practiced there. Indeed, most of the largest religions originated there.

Yet, for all its diversity, family is the concept that binds Asians together, as it does in other parts of the world. The notion of family in East Asia is shaped by the Confucian culture. In these countries particularly, family as an idea is the cornerstone on which society is built.

According to Confucian teachings, there is no peace in the world without peace in the family. In Korea, there is a proverb: *Gahwamahnsasung*, this is composed of five Chinese letters, 家和萬事成, "ga" as family, "hwa" as peace, "mahn" literally 10,000 but generally meaning a lot of everything, "sa" as work, and "sung" as done well, or done successfully.

This basically means "all will be well when family is well." "All will be at peace when family is at peace."

Family is like glue that sticks us together. Family members know instinctively that the well-being of one is dependent on the well-being of others. This is a truth we all have been living out during these months in the era of the COVID-19 outbreak with the slogan, "We are all in this together." It is also a teaching of indigenous people who speak of *kahkiyaw niwâhkômâkanitik* (ᑲᐦᑭᔭᐤ ᓂᐚᐦᑰᒫᑲᓂᑎᐠ) "All my Relations" in the Cree language, you and me, that plant, that tree, that bird. We are all bound together into family.

As family we sacrifice for one another. Sacrifice in the Bible means giving burned offerings to God. That is what we heard in the Psalm today. It is a time to make sacrifices. It is a time to make fire, create smoke, burn the incense, and invoke God in prayer. It is a time to pray for one another. Psalm 141 connects the act of burning incense with prayer. The smoke in the air symbolizes and connects the dead and the living, our extended family bound together. Many of you have not seen your family who are on the other side of the globe. Some of you have been unable to visit your loved ones even if they are close to you geographically.

In this difficult heartbreaking situation, Jesus offers these comforting words, "If you remain in me and my words remain in you, ask whatever you wish, and it will be done for you." "Jesus is the vine and we are his branches." This language of John conjures up the image of the bound family vine. What I mean by this is that, as a family, it is like a vine of branches that intertwine and wrap around one another, and that have the same source of life. We are all children of God. We belong to one family vine in God's sight. In this sense, we are bound. We are like a family vine bound together.

The Gospel of John speaks a language akin to the Confucian language of family. I can imagine John and Confucius over tea swapping ideas in conversation, John telling Confucius that his teacher, Jesus, called God *Abba*, an intimate father, parental figure, whose place as the progenitor of the whole family teaches us that we are all relations.

The writer of the Gospel of John, who in addition to the Gospel, also wrote three letters, spoke in a passionate way about love as he understood it as a Christian. Among all four Gospels, John is the one who talks about love most strongly. It is understandable because John's community was a precarious minority Christian community facing severe persecution. In their time of danger, love was what kept them together. Like John's Christian community, our own community feels precarious and afraid in this time of the COVID-19 global pandemic. John says to his community that love casts out fear.

Our world today is faced with serious challenges. Many families are suffering on multiple levels. Many of us feel lost at home, at school, at work, and even at church. The slaves on the American plantations used to sing, "Sometimes I feel like a motherless child, a long way from home."[38]

What feeling can be worse than being separated from one's mother? So often it can feel that we have been separated from our family, from our sources of support and encouragement. It can feel like the very cords binding us to life have been severed. And survival seems like a distant and fading hope. In that moment, the Spirit appears as *The Paraclete*, the Greek word translated as "Advocate," or "Helper" in English. When we feel utterly helpless, the Spirit of God helps us and we can sometimes feel that help. This Advocate-Spirit is not a meek assistant. Jesus told the disciples and we heard it today for ourselves: "I will not leave you orphaned! You will not be without family." Jesus uses the language of family. The Advocate-Spirit of God evokes the bonds of family connecting us to a mother, to a home, to a community. It is the spiritual tie that binds us, one to the other, all our relations, *kahkiyaw niwâhkômâkanitik*.

Even if we are asked not to visit friends or family, even when we are asked to self-quarantine, even when we are prevented from seeing loved ones in a long term care home, even when we are separated from a job and a secure income, even when we witness or are the victims of prejudice and racism, even when the world seems to be churning with fear and danger, we are not alone. God is such an awesome God, our advocate, our protector, who will not leave us orphaned.

The impact of this global pandemic is unknown. We cannot see where it is going. We cannot see when it will end. The world as we know it is unraveling. One troubling aspect of this is the working conditions of our cleaners and janitors, our essential workers. They are invisible to most of us most of the time because they work at night when we all go home to our comfortable places to rest after work. These invisible workers are predominantly women, and many of them are recent immigrants, and most of them are from Asia. Some are undocumented workers, and don't even have a valid Social Insurance Number. This means they do not receive any benefits. It means they don't get paid sick days and extra work hours. Most of them are contract workers and don't have proper health and safety equipment to protect themselves from getting this virus. And yet they have no choice but to work to put food on the table for their family. In many cases, they are not legally and medically protected at all. Ironically, however, these most vulnerable family members of our society are looking after us. They are the ones who protect the health of the public. They are the ones who sanitize places so that we can safely commute, shop, work, and get medical help in this scary COVID-19 virus spreading world. In the process, they put themselves at risk. They sacrifice.

These women and men from Asia and other parts of the world are part of our Canadian family. Our country Canada is a big vine with many different branches. Their work and courage are the lifeblood that courses through our veins and helps us to carry on. We must not stop that lifeblood from circulating back to them. Through this crisis and afterward, our hearts must continue to pump blood to them, recognizing them and fighting for fair conditions for them. After all, we belong to one bound family vine. Their branches are bound with ours. We intertwine. We are glued to each other.

Gawhamansasung. All will be well when family is well. Jesus offers again, "If you remain in me and my words remain in you, ask whatever you wish, and it will be done for you." When people take care of people, I feel the life-giving sap coursing through the roots and up to the branches. I see the new buds bursting open on the branches and vines of this bound family. Can you see them too? That is the vision of Easter, the sign of new life, and the beauty of a bound family vine.

NOTES

1. R. S. Sugirtharajah, "Afterword: Cultures, Texts and Margins: A Hermeneutical Odyssey," in *Voices from the Margins*, 460.

2. Barbara Brown Taylor, "Preaching the Body," in *Listening to the Word: Studies in Honor of Fred B. Craddock*, ed. Gail R. O'Day & Thomas G. Long (Nashville: Abingdon, 1993), 210–211.

3. Taylor, "Preaching the Body," 214.

4. Dietrich Bonhoeffer, *Worldly Preaching* (New York: Thomas Nelson, 1975), 16.

5. Henry Mitchell, "The Hearer's Experience of the Word," in *Listening to the Word: Studies in Honor of Fred B. Craddock*, ed. Gail R. O'Day and Thomas G. Long (Nashville: Abingdon, 1993), 231.

6. Teresa Fry Brown, *Delivering the Sermon: Voice, Body, and Animation in Proclamation* (Minneapolis: Fortress, 2008), 18–19.

7. LaRue, *The Heart of Black Preaching*, 10.

8. Richard Ward, *Speaking of the Holy: The Art of Communication in Preaching* (St. Louis: Chalice, 2001), 38–39.

9. Fry Brown, *Delivering the Sermon*, 64.

10. Kathy Black, *A Healing Homiletic: Preaching ad Disability* (Nashville: Abingdon, 1996), 100.

11. Allen, "The Social Function of Language in Preaching," 167.

12. Ossie Davis, "The English Language is My Enemy," in *Revelations: An Anthology of Expository Essays by and about Blacks*, ed. Teresa M. Reed (Needham Heights: Ginn Press, 1991), 163–164.

13. David M. Goldenberg, *The Curse of Ham: Race and Slavery in Early Judaism, Christianity, and Islam* (New Jersey: Princeton University Press, 2005).

14. Stephen R. Haynes, *Noah's Curse: The Biblical Justification of American Slavery* (Oxford: Oxford University Press, 2002).

15. Phyllis Trible, *God and the Rhetoric of Sexuality* (Philadelphia: Fortress, 1978), 72–143. Carol Meyers, *Discovering Eve: Ancient Israelite Women in Context* (Oxford: Oxford University Press, 2013).

16. Allen, "The Social Function of Language in Preaching," 171, 174.

17. Christine Smith, *Preaching as Weeping, Confession, and Resistance: Radical Response to Radical Evil* (Louisville: Westminster John Knox 1992), 131.

18. Allen, "The Social Function of Language in Preaching," 181.

19. Ibid., 175.

20. Kenneth Burke, *A Grammar of Motives* (Berkeley: University of California Press, 1959), 3–9, cited in Richard Lischer, "Preaching as the Church's Language," in *Interpreting to the Word: Studies in Honor of Fred B. Craddock*, ed. Gail R. O'Day and Thomas Long (Nashville: Abingdon, 1993), 117.

21. Lischer, "Preaching as the Church's Language," 117.

22. Ibid., 126.

23. Nieman and Rogers, *Preaching to Every Pew*, 35.

24. Kim, "The World of Ethnic and Cultural Issues in Preaching," 85–86.

25. Boyung Lee, *Transforming Congregations through Community: Faith Formation from the Seminary to the Church* (Louisville: Westminster John Knox, 2013), 3, 8.

26. Nieman and Rogers, *Preaching to Every Pew*, 24.

27. Smith, *Preaching as Weeping, Confession, and Resistance*, 131.

28. Kim, "The World of Ethnic and Cultural Issues in Preaching," 74.

29. Matthew D. Kim, "A Blindspot in Homiletics: Preaching That Exegetes Ethnicity," *Journal of the Evangelical Homiletics Society* 11:1 (March 2011): 66–83.

30. John D. Frederick Lugard, *The Dual Mandate in British Tropical Africa* (Edinburgh: Blackwood, 1922), 618–619.

31. Robert J. C. Young, *Colonial Desire: Hybridity in Theory, Culture and Race* (London: Routledge, 1995), 29–89.

32. Ibid., 31.

33. Ibid., 43.

34. Ibid., 31.

35. Ibid., 52.

36. Patricia Seed, *Ceremonies of Possession in Europe's Conquest of the New World, 1492–1640* (Cambridge: Cambridge University Press, 1995).

37. Richard Eslinger, *A New Hearing: Living Options in Homiletic Method* (Minneapolis: Fortress, 1987), 139.

38. https://www.youtube.com/watch?v=F3oVz1Wjb7w

Chapter 6

Exegesis

Exploring a Postcolonial Contrapuntal Reading for Interpreting Scripture

When he came to Nazareth, where he had been brought up, he went to the synagogue on the sabbath day, as was his custom. He stood up to read, and the scroll of the prophet Isaiah was given to him. He unrolled the scroll and found the place where it was written: "The Spirit of the Lord is upon me, because he has anointed me to bring good news to the poor. He has sent me to proclaim release to the captives and recovery of sight to the blind, to let the oppressed go free, to proclaim the year of the Lord's favor." And he rolled up the scroll, gave it back to the attendant, and sat down. The eyes of all in the synagogue were fixed on him. Then he began to say to them, "Today this scripture has been fulfilled in your hearing."

—Luke 4: 16:21

The Gospel of Luke records Jesus's real-time exegesis of Isa. 61:1–2 and the scandal it created. Jesus's interpretation directly challenged the status quo and threatened the privilege of the powerful. One may argue that Jesus's exegesis was his first step on the way to the cross. It is obvious that the way we interpret scripture for preaching matters. The way we interpret the text is even, at times, a matter of life and death. In this final chapter, we will explore Exegesis in the RIPPLE effect and attempt to round off this preliminary sketch of postcolonial homiletics. Exegesis is as crucial to preaching as the battery is to a car engine; to preach without exegeting scripture, is like thinking one can start a car without the battery. As a spark, exegesis arouses curiosity. It inspires. It troubles. And it moves.

To exegete texts in the Bible for postcolonial preaching is to spark an interaction between the words of scripture and our present postcolonial struggles, and also to move us to participate in those struggles. The postcolonial preacher knows that every book of the Bible from Genesis to Revelation contains colonial experiences. Each story is touched by actions of various empires: Egypt, Assyria, Babylon, Persia, Greece, and Rome. What I contend is that every preacher who mounts the pulpit, or faces a congregation, or seeks to share in any venue the Word of God in the twenty-first century, needs to be a postcolonial preacher. The interplay among text, preacher, and the congregation as reflective of the contemporary cultural context is crucial for homiletical exegesis. Scripture contains a similar dynamic. The Bible was primarily an oral product at the confluence of author/speaker, people as community of faith, and cultural context. Exegesis is about interpreting the biblical text and that of the situation of the congregation so that the Word can be affirmed as dwelling among them. The Greek word for "dwelt," *skenow*, is the same word used in the Septuagint (Greek translation of Hebrew Bible) for "tabernacle." The tabernacle is a mobile tent for worship and sacrifice, for people of Jewish faith. It is at the heart of Judaism in the life of the diasporas. The tabernacle physically and visibly reminded the wandering Hebrews of God's presence wherever they went, as they also carried the Word with them. The journey continued when it reminded John within his early Christian community that the Word became flesh and "dwelt" among us (John 1:14). The writer of the Gospel of John, for the Jewish minoritized Christian community, is recalling the cultural context of the Hebrew tradition. Fred Craddock put it this way, "the way of God's Word in the world is the way of the sermon in the world."[1]

This chapter will tackle postcolonial exegetical issues in four steps. First, we will critically examine the dominant exegetical approach in the pulpit today, known as historical criticism. Second, we will explain an important strategy at the heart of postcolonial exegesis, something called contrapuntal reading. Third, we will test out our postcolonial approach on various Bible passages. Finally, we will present a sermon of Pablo Jiménez as an example that highlights a postcolonial exegetical method of a contrapuntal reading.

Effective scriptural exegesis for preaching in a postcolonial context cannot happen if the reader/preacher does not understand and reflect upon the colonial realities, which are at the core of the biblical witness. Leaving the colonial issues out of biblical exegesis for preachers who seek to address issues of racial injustice is like fish trying to swim out of water, or a baker trying to make the bread rise without yeast. Yet, most well-funded commentaries have not sufficiently paid attention to colonial conditions and their impact upon the people of faith in the Bible. Between historical criticism on one end of the spectrum, and biblical literalism on the other end, power differentials in the text are buried. Colonial problems embedded in the Bible must be more daringly exposed, and more vigorously expounded as an essential part of any homiletical exegesis. Historical biblical criticism has been such a dominant tool in twentieth century homiletical exegesis. Part of the reason that not much attention has been paid to postcolonial issues in our commentaries is the absence of well-developed postcolonial reading strategies. Utilizing the work of Edward Said, I propose a contrapuntal approach to reading scripture. Exegesis, using the contrapuntal method, allows preachers to zoom in on the colonial experiences that exist in and between the lines of text. This method is particularly helpful for uncovering otherwise hidden and unspoken colonial contexts and experiences in the Bible. Once these colonial experiences are unearthed, it is possible for preachers to address the current postcolonial concerns of their congregation directly from the Bible. Seen within the colonial context, preachers are better equipped to bear faithful witness and to proclaim God's favor as Jesus did (Luke 4:19).

Once we have introduced a contrapuntal reading strategy, we will attempt to exegete narratives in Exodus, the story of Rahab in Joshua, some stories of Jesus in the Gospels, and some passages in Paul's letters. These texts have been selected for attention here because they prominently feature complicated relationships and identities directly related to postcolonial conditions dealing with institutional violence, slavery, gender, authority, citizenship, ethnicity, race, and class. These texts, therefore, provide close-ups of the colonial realities, which are prevalent in the Bible. Finally, the sermon example provided will demonstrate how a contrapuntal reading strategy can effectively incorporate a subaltern perspective for a postcolonial preaching approach.

A POSTCOLONIAL CRITIQUE OF HISTORICAL BIBLICAL CRITICISM

The historical criticism method in biblical studies emerged in Europe in the nineteenth century among the work of Germans, English, and French scholars. As a product of the Enlightenment faith in reason, historical criticism was contemporaneous to the rise of Western science and expansion of European empires. Historical criticism, particularly at the beginning, assumed a white male preacher who subscribed to the scientific values of impartiality and objectivity when interpreting the Bible. The approach was inherently colonialist and imperialistic. Fernando Segovia, a biblical scholar, points out that historical criticism

> unreflectively universalized its bracketed identity, expecting on the surface all readers everywhere to become ideal critics . . . while its actuality required all readers to interpret like European critics. In fact, the entire discussion . . . was characterized and governed by the fundamental questions . . . of this particular

group, uncritically disguised as the fundamental questions of the entire Christian world.... The result was a classic case of neocolonialism, where the interests of the colonized or the margins were sacrificed, subtly but surely, to the interests of the colonizers or the center.[2]

Segovia goes to the heart of the issue. Historical criticism, as a child of its context, was oblivious to many of the issues that are central to postcolonial thought. The supposed objectivity of historical criticism was imbued with its bias in favor of European empire, subject to the underlying assumption of white supremacy promoted by those empires and oblivious to the plight of the colonized. This tradition of criticism, therefore, while providing some helpful tools for understanding the Bible that contributed to a critical homiletical approach in Europe and North America, is unequipped to deal with postcolonial concerns. Many of these postcolonial concerns are bound to be political and visceral. Historical criticism ignores these difficult realities and allows preaches a way to escape having to address them. Justo Gonzalez, a historian who has written preaching books, bluntly criticizes North American pulpits that uncritically opt for historical criticism, because the pulpits become an enslaved place, which is "tied to modern paradigms of supposed objectivity, chained to a shallow scientism that often translate into psychologism." In this idolatrous affair of historical biblical criticism, he writes, "Scripture . . . is tamed into a book of religious observances, moral platitudes, and psychological banalities."[3]

Since the days of the prophets, scriptural exegesis has been highly political. Its approaches to interpretations helped unearth the hidden power in the Bible to confront the status quo and transform the social reality. To interpret the Bible in this way requires the courage to swim against the current. Biblical scholar Mary Ann Tolbert admits that it is far easier to read from the perspective of power, "Not only do the 'canonical' texts of Western culture communicate hierarchical values and androcentric worldviews, but the very conventions of good reading taught within the culture encourage their acceptance."[4] Minoritized scholars in North America know only all too well the challenges involved in opposing the status quo. The conventional approach to the Bible in the academy has entrenched historical criticism and has made it difficult for those who do not conform to the white, male, Western-language-speaking norm to insert themselves and assert the concerns coming from their marginalized contexts.[5]

The critique of historical criticism has been coupled with preaching the objective truth. Austin Phelps, who wrote the standard textbook for preaching classes in the late nineteenth and the early twentieth century, portrayed the preacher as a well-armed gunner who must know what and where the vulnerable spots are. He is talking about the vulnerable spots as the heathens whom preacher should aim at. Armed with the truth, he writes, preachers are "manly clergy" who "make the pulpit the place where their strength [is] expended."[6] Such an example highlights the powerful masculine character of the preacher, whose job it is to target and demolish opposing views. The portrayal of the preacher in such militaristic terms serves to justify an aggressive approach toward those who may be different, religiously, culturally, or racially.

Influenced by modernist thought, the puritan style dominated preaching in the Americas from the nineteenth into the early twentieth century. "Collectively, over the span of the colonial era, New England ministers delivered . . . five million sermons, each sixty to ninety minutes long . . . . But even more significant than the frequency of sermon delivery was the fact that the sermon, considered a medium of public communication, had no competition . . . . New England Puritans invested the sermon with a monolithic voice that spoke authoritatively to every significant event in the life of the community."[7] John Albert Broadus (1827–1895) of the United States in his *On the Preparation and Delivery of Sermons* (1870) made North American expository preaching more argumentative and less an analysis of the text.[8] Naming the influence of Broadus's book, Lucy A. Rose writes, his "textbook defined preaching for the first half of the twentieth century."[9] Rose argues that though much has changed in recent years, much has also remained the same. The historicizing tendency is a weakness of the expository preaching style that should not be ignored. Without reflecting their own place and time, the preacher "lives with Elijah in the cave on Horeb rather than in the suburb where his [sic] congregants dwell."[10] It becomes even more problematic, when the past filled with colonial violence is forgotten and left uncontested.

There are a couple of postcolonial optics that help confront these difficulties with alternative ways of readings the Bible. One is a "culturally treasonable" approach. Tolbert suggests that a culturally treasonable way of reading questions what is sometimes assumed to be a "natural" interpretation. This requires learning a particular skill in order to recognize the hegemony embedded in the text. Those with that skill become "resistant readers" betraying "conventional rules devised by the cultural elite of any literate society."[11] When the text says, "slaves obey your masters" or "women must be silent in church," a culturally treasonable reading simply turns its back on the claim, and instead de-normalizes readings that seek to normalize slavery and sexism as if they are natural. Biblical stories of sexual violence and war, for example, if normalized, fail to acknowledge the victims or to seek out their perspectives of events, perspectives that may contribute to healing. To avoid the pitfalls of normalizing what should not be normalized, preachers must anchor themselves in the wisdom that affirms the dignity of life and seeks to give voice to the voiceless. Heeding the advice of Segovia and Tolbert, preachers will need to dig deep within themselves to be prepared to be traitors for the sake of bearing witness to the Gospel.

The second postcolonial optic is the affirmation that while all knowledge is perspectival, not all perspectives are equally valid.[12] This relativist claim has been criticized by postcolonial marginalized social groups, because it fails to reveal the unequal social structures, which are already encoded and masked behind the rhetoric of truth, meaning, and justice. Postcolonial theorist Stephen Slemon argues that "an interested postcolonial critical practice would want to allow for the positive production of oppositional truth-claims in these texts." A postcolonial reading, he continues, retains "a mimetic or referential purchase to textuality, and it would recognize in this referential drive the operations of a critical strategy for survival in marginalized social groups."[13] To claim that knowledge is perspectival acknowledges that perspectives are power-laden. Perspectives, in other words, cannot escape one's sociopolitical economic and cultural locations, as discussed in chapter 3 on the preaching place. Liberation theology's preferential option for the poor is a case in point. The "poor" in postcolonial theory are not limited to those marginalized in an economic and material sense, though these conditions are an essential measure of marginalization. The poor can also refer to those who are marginalized due to their identities or multiple and shifting positions within the dominant culture. The voices of the poor point to the marginalized voices including but not limited to nonwhite, women, non-Anglo voices. In the 1980s, many of these voices began to make themselves heard in the North American academy and in biblical and theological disciplines. Ironically, this decade also saw the rise of deconstructionist thought, which argued no voice or perspective should be given a greater degree of legitimacy or weight in interpreting a given text. This deconstructionist approach, when it is taken too rigidly, had the effect of silencing minority voices, just as they were beginning to be heard. The attempt of anyone including the minority to offer a textual reading is deconstructed and even dismissed as theoretically unsound, as Tolbert observes, thus, "allowing the conventional interpretations of elite male scholars to reign supreme by default."[14] The postcolonial optic must insist postcolonial observations not be dismissed or downplayed by both objective and relativist discourses. For feminists, it is legitimate to make a universal claim of women's oppression because patriarchy is real and prevalent. In other words, when a community justifies stoning a woman to death because she has been accused of engaging in sexual intercourse outside of marriage, the language of moral outrage is justified that such actions are simply, objectively, and universally wrong.[15] Yet, violence against women is complex and its root causes are often intersectional and include vectors of sexuality, economy, religion, and culture. Addressing women's issues, like any other issues, therefore, requires forming strategic coalitions and nuancing complicated situations between different marginalized groups. Such coalitions are part of the postcolonial optic when approaching the Bible as well.

THE CONTRAPUNTAL READING STRATEGY

The contrapuntal reading strategy was suggested by Edward Said, a literary critic of Palestinian background who blazed the trail for postcolonial thought in the late twentieth century. The contrapuntal reading strategy insists that when one interprets colonial texts whether literary, scientific, or religious, the perspective of the colonizer and the colonized must be considered. Said's main interests were the study of novels published by subjects of the British and French Empires of the eighteenth and nineteenth centuries. However, the strategy he developed may also be applied to Christianity's sacred texts. These texts were written and were later also interpreted, in colonial environments and so it follows that, like texts written in the context of modern imperial expansion, the same technique may be applied.

Reading contrapuntally means taking account of different perspectives simultaneously and seeing how the text interacts with historical or biographical contexts. Said notes a contrapuntal reading is reading with "awareness both of the metropolitan history that is narrated and of those other histories against which (and together with which) the dominating discourse acts."[16] This is a reading tool to make visible that which is invisible to the characters in the novel and often the authors themselves. Contrapuntal reading relies upon the reader's ability to provide the context, which will make subaltern (meaning oppressed, suppressed, minoritized, and marginalized) experiences perceptible, intertwined as they are with the experience of the colonizer. The goal of a contrapuntal reading is not to be content with the dominant and obvious point of view (which is often what the author explicitly provides in the story) but to reveal the hidden issues of the colonized that are intermeshed and embedded in the text. It is to make the absence of the colonized present.

Jacques Derrida, the philosopher and theorist, also spoke of the significance of what is absent in a text.[17] This is a paradox of hermeneutics. One is expected to notice a presence because of its absence. Derrida's attention to absences further contributes to our appreciation of Said's contrapuntal insights.

The term "contrapuntal" has also been deployed by homiletician David Buttrick who introduced the same term in his discussion of sermonic moves. For Buttrick, the contrapuntal statement in a sermon creates room for doubt and questions.[18] It must be noted that his use of contrapuntal is different from that of Said. However, there is a point of similarity in that it opens a space to consider questions that might not otherwise be raised. Said wants to create an opening between the surface meaning of a text and the colonial context, which is often left unsaid, to allow reflection upon what has been taken for granted and left unexamined. In his examination of Jane Austen's novel *Mansfield Park* (1814), for example, Said notes that a family is featured whose wealth derives from a sugar plantation in Antigua.[19] While there is no mention of Antigua in the novel, the reader, employing a contrapuntal strategy, can use his or her knowledge of the colonial context to interpret the story of this family in the light of the structural dependency of his or her family upon the colonies. In the case of *Mansfield Park*, though the action of the story takes place in London, far removed from the colonies, a contrapuntal reading brings to consciousness what is happening in the faraway colonies as necessary context in understanding the story.

With postcolonial imagination employing a contrapuntal reading strategy, readers can detect the silenced voices of those struggling under colonial structures. What is not said may be as important as what is said. Through the contrapuntal strategy, the reader can nuance the text "with an understanding of what is involved when an author shows, for instance, that a colonial sugar plantation is seen as important to the process of maintaining a particular style of life in England."[20] For Said, a contrapuntal reading helps to identify distinct, albeit silenced, voices, while bringing them into conversation with the overt colonizer perspective that silenced them. This contrapuntal interpretive method provides an insight for postcolonial hermeneutics; a vision that recognizes differences, detects muted sounds, and unmasks power differentials toward proclaiming the good news of a more balanced and transformed relationship.

Said's astute interdisciplinary approach provides tools for those who wish to read the Bible for preaching in a postcolonial way. Through the contrapuntal approach are we able to hear voices silenced by the authors, redactors, and interpreters through the years. Exegeting the Bible contrapuntally means exposing the truth through awareness of the patterns of power and domination embedded in scripture.

CONTRAPUNTAL EXEGESES OF THE BIBLE

A homiletical use of the contrapuntal approach focuses on what I call the "3 B" principles: the world *behind* the text, the world *between* the text and the world *before* the text.[21] Historical criticism helps us see *behind* the text by focusing on the authorship, the date of the composition of a text and giving it historical context. Critical methods, including structuralism, narrative, literary, and rhetorical criticisms for preaching pay attention to meanings *between* the text. Finally, feminist criticism, cultural hermeneutics, postcolonial criticism, reader-response criticism, womanist criticism, and deconstruction perspectives help the preacher address the world *before* the text.

Until recently, the world behind the text has received the lion's share of the attention from scholars and homileticians. Historical criticism's contribution to a postcolonial exegesis has to do with its demonstration of "the worldliness" of the Bible; the ideological, religious, and material background that helps us see the text as part of an historical process. But while one unveils the ancient world behind the text, historical criticism neglects to disclose the contemporary world that the preacher belongs to and fails to draw connections between the two worlds relevant to the postcolonial challenges facing the church today.

The problem lies within historical criticism when the world/author of the text is divorced from the reader. This divorce becomes hegemonic when we readers ignore the fact that the editing and selection process was imbued with androcentric, patriarchal, and hierarchical biases. It is generally accepted that most writers of the Bible, interpreters, and editors of the canonization of the Bible were elite, male, religious leaders. They were culturally bounded and politically charged. The canonization was, hence, never neutral. Yet, what historical criticism has done successfully is that it "deliberately bracketed the social location of those who [wrote], read and interpreted the work," as if they lived outside culture.[22] To unbracket that in reading the Bible is to read it in culturally treasonable ways, as discussed earlier. Our job as postcolonial readers of the Bible includes exposing the authors' epistemological biases and limitations.

Rahab in Exodus and Joshua

With the three B basic exegetical components in mind—*behind, between, before*—we will scrutinize some of the colonial experiences deposited in the text of the Bible. In doing so, we feature specific texts dealing with slavery, gender, conquest, and displacement starting with the story of Rahab in the Book of Joshua. The story of the Exodus is foundational to Jewish and Christian traditions. It is the story of the Hebrews, ancestors of the people of Israel who were slaves in Egypt searching for freedom and a land to call their own. This story is the central focus of the Torah, the five most foundational books in Judaism. Following the order of the Christian canon, the Exodus, which is the focus of the first five books, culminates in the sixth book, Joshua, which tells the story of the Israelites finally conquering and occupying Canaan. The story of Exodus is a pivotal narrative serving as the cornerstone of Christian liberation theology. In the story of the Exodus, God hears the cries and sees the misery of the enslaved Hebrews. God calls upon Moses, God's servant, to go to Egypt and tell Pharaoh, "Let my people go!"

(3:6–5:1). Latin American liberation theology along with Minjung, Feminist, and womanist theologies, claims that God is liberator; God takes the side with the oppressed.

Yet, God's resounding command through the voice of Moses to "let my people go" is, according to Musa Dube, "unhesitatingly twined with God's promise to give them the land of the Canaanites, the Hittites, the Amorites, the Perizzites, the Hivites, and the Jebusites—an inhabited land!"[23] From these inhabitant's perspectives, God's promise to the people of Israel signifies not liberation but invasion and conquest, the removal of their land. As Paulo Freire writes, "every hypertrophy somewhere in the system provokes atrophy somewhere else."[24] What he implies is that privilege is earned at the cost of the exploitation and at the expense of others. It is hard to reconcile God's promise to the Israelites, with the invasion and conquest of other peoples. One way people have tried to come to terms with this is to imagine that for one reason or another the Canaanites don't count as people. This interpretation has had major consequences for world history. Indeed, such a perspective is reflected in the history of modern colonialism, when the Pope, in 1493, declared that land occupied in the "New World" by non-Christians was in fact *terra nullius* in Latin literally means "nobody's land" or "empty land." From this idea emerged the Pope's Doctrine of Discovery, declaring that Spain and Portugal were entitled to claim through colonial conquest the land on which indigenous people in America lived. Because indigenous peoples were non-Christians, the Pope considered them as nobodies. They were not counted as people, and by implication, the people there could be exterminated or enslaved. The Doctrine of Discovery provided a framework for European Christian colonialists to lay claim to the land and bodies of others. During the period of modern colonialism, the Bible was used as a tool to conquer many parts of the world. Such faith stories as those in Exodus and Joshua have fueled the political rhetoric of conquest.[25]

For this reason, Christian preachers must wrestle with the Exodus story, its complexities, and its tensions. A postcolonial reading allows them to place the Bible within a colonial context and in conversation with the current postcolonial reality. Preachers cannot play innocent; nor can they deny the reality of conquest. In fact, the denial of conquest has often been used in colonial literature and its interpretation. Mary Louise Pratt coined the term "anti-conquest" as a pattern in the literature of imperial settings that establishes the colonizers' innocence in the occupation of the land and the assertion of their right to travel to, enter, and possess them.[26] Dube contends that the construction of the innocence of the colonizers is followed by three movements in colonial literature. First, images of the targeted land and its people are constructed in order to justify their conquest. Second, the identity of the people who colonize distant lands is constructed to justify their displacement of others. Finally, a construction of female gender is used to articulate relations of subjugation and domination.[27]

The story of Rahab in Joshua exactly follows Dube's three stages of an anti-conquest narrative. First, the image is established: the land of milk and honey. This is a desirable and inviting land. It is occupied land. The Exodus narrative is painfully honest on this fact (Exod. 3:8, 17; 6:4; 13:5, 23:23; 33:2), but the people are unworthy, it is implied, because they do not worship God (Exod. 23:23). The Hebrews are therefore justified to enter the land, occupy it, and "blot out" the inhabitants. They are "ungodly," thus their practices ought to be destroyed: "you shall utterly destroy them and break their pillars in pieces" (23:24). This sets up the second movement of the story, which is that the Israelites are innocent victims of the Egyptian empire and in need of a home. What is more, they worship "the true God." The special identity of the people of Israel as God's chosen race, signified as "the firstborn son" (4:22), is established. While the inhabitant people are barbaric and ungodly, the people of Israel are innocent and holy, the rightful heirs of God's land. The third and final device has to do with the feminization of the colonized. Here Rahab, the woman prostitute, represents Canaan. The colonized portrayed as a prostitute is a debased group of people. As female, they also have less authority and strength and therefore require a masculine people to come in and take charge.

The story of Rahab takes a further twist, which is possible to appreciate only with a postcolonial lens. If we read contrapuntally, it becomes apparent that Rahab serves as "the mouthpiece" of the colonizer's fantasy, that the colonized will voluntarily proclaim the colonizer's victory, and pledge absolute loyalty. But Laura Donaldson, an indigenous postcolonial scholar, suggests that if we "read like a Canaanite," the conversion of Rahab rings hallow.[28] Stepping into the shoes of a Canaanite, one can imagine the feelings of loss and the tears that must have been shed by the inhabitants of Jericho. In this imaginative and emphatic process, the hidden and the ambivalent sides are exposed in Joshua. The story of Rahab can be an effective prism for a decolonizing and anti-patriarchal biblical exegesis and can advance strategic intersecting justice initiatives in the postcolonial era.[29]

Jesus' Use of Abba in the Gospels

The four Gospels in the Christian scriptures all depict the life, suffering, death, and resurrection of Jesus. These Gospels are followed by the epistles, including the letters of Paul, addressed to and written out of the early church communities. The Christian Testament concludes with Revelation, a book written by John (and his community) exiled on the Island of Patmos who is greatly distressed by the colonizing powers at work in the land. John deemed as the author of this book denounced the empire, including the imperial cult, urging his community to come out of the colonial power by excoriating it as Satanic exploitation and resisting.[30] These texts as well as acts and the non-Pauline letters are all written from within the context of the Roman Empire. Every book in the Christian Testament contains the voices of the colonized and is shaped by the context of colonization. With this in mind, the name that Jesus uses for God takes on special significance.

From the feminist point of view, Jesus's reference to God as *Abba* (father in Aramaic) has never been easy to accept. Its translation, as *Pater* in Greek and later "Father" in English, has been used as an authoritative utterance to establish a male-dominant theology and to justify patriarchy since the earliest days of Christianity. Vigorous feminist critiques have challenged the obviously sexist interpretation, which assigns God an exclusively male gender. However, a contrapuntal reading of Jesus's name for God within the context of the Roman imperial theology offers a refreshing insight into its significance for Jesus' time and for our own. Mary Rose D' Angelo agrees that the use of "father" as a name for God is patriarchal and is not liberating for women[31] but she points out that the title of "Father" was used throughout the Roman Empire to refer to Julius Caesar. *Pater* reflects "an understanding of the empire as a great *familia* in which the emperor functions as a *paterfamilias* whose *auctoritas* is based on his ability to regard the whole Roman people as his clients."[32] Jesus's particular use of God as *Abba*, however, implicitly displaces Caesar from the top of the hierarchy. In addition, the intimate nature of the term *Abba* challenges the distant and formal imperial authority connoted by "Father." This is a good example of a contrapuntal exegesis of the Bible because the connection between *Abba*, the name Jesus used to address God, and *Pater*, the *paterfamilias* notion of Julius Caesar is nowhere made explicit in the text. The reference leaves a trace of itself not only in its counter-correspondence to the imperial idea but also through its use of the Aramaic language, the language of the colonized, in contradiction to Latin or Hellenistic Greek, the languages of the colonizers. Furthermore, the decolonizing interpretation of *Abba* is supported by other passages in the Christian scriptures when Jesus confronts the Roman Empire in a clever yet indirect way, calling on the Israelites to give to Caesar what belongs to Caesar and to God what belongs to God (Mark 12:17). In short, Jesus's utterance of *Abba*, in calling upon God, exposes Caesar's heretical claim to authority, while lifting up the voices of the colonized, the Aramaic voices that counter the voice of domination, submission, and subversion. The sound of the Aramaic word for "Dad" rings with a note of resistance.[33] This exegesis of Jesus's use of the name *Abba* for God not only challenges the status quo but also offers us a model of exegesis for postcolonial preaching.

The Epistles of Paul in Gal. 4:21–31 and 1 Cor. 6: 15–20

The impact of the theology that Paul develops in his epistles is immense and has been the focus of biblical studies and homiletics throughout Christian history. While his prominence in Christian preaching is unequalled, Christian interpretations of Paul's views about things from women to slavery and from marriage to sexuality are far from unanimous and remain controversial. Paul was a complicated person with multiple hybrid identities. One might say that he is an ideal postcolonial subject. He was a Greek-speaking Jew. He was a Pharisee, yet dedicated his life to work with the gentiles who were unwelcome among his fellow Judeans. He was a free-born well-educated privileged male who held Roman citizenship, and therefore had the right to own slaves. His original name was Jewish, Saul. Later, he adopted the Hellenistic name, Paul. He willingly joined the ranks of a community that was being persecuted. He could have enjoyed all his privileges and continued to live life persecuting them from his safe perch atop the imperial hierarchy.[34] Instead, he ended up being persecuted by the Roman Empire and, in the end, died as a colonized Jew. Paul's complex life with his hybrid identities sheds light on the significance of the social location of preachers as discussed in chapter 3, something that contemporary preachers who aspire to be relevant to the postcolonial context need to grapple with as well.

For our purpose, a contrapuntal exegesis of Galatians 4 and 1 Corinthians 6 yields insights for addressing the colonial realities of slavery, gender, race, ethnicity, sexuality, and religion, all of which constitute a "multiaxial frame of reference" in postcolonial biblical studies and preaching.[35] Most of all, the text from Galatians that deals with slavery and the comparison of Sarah and Hagar as symbols of two covenants complicates the claim that Paul's is an anti-imperial stance. In this passage, for example, he does not condemn the institution of slavery sanctioned by the imperial order. This chapter 4 of Galatians is particularly puzzling because it comes right after the most well-known baptismal formula of 3:26–28, "there is no longer Greek or Jew, there is no longer free or slave, there is no longer male and female, for all of you are one in Christ Jesus." Hence, Paul seems to contradict himself. We are not sure if he supports or is opposed to the institution of slavery. It is also problematic because his interpretation of Hagar as cursed and unworthy of the inheritance of God's promise does not reflect the blessing found in the Hebrew Bible. For it is clear she received a blessing from God in Genesis (16:10, 21:18). A simple intertextual reading shows that Paul neglects all positive aspects of the amazing encounter between God and Hagar in the wilderness. Paul's favoring of Sarah over Hagar and Sarah's children against Hagar's children has had grave consequences in the history of religion. It has not only suggested the superiority of Christianity over Judaism but also later contributed to divisions between Christianity and Islam. Christians, both boastfully and shamefully, regarded themselves as the more favorable descendants of Abraham and Sarah. Muslims, as the descendants of Hagar are thought not to deserve God's blessing. While it is impossible to fully know what Paul intended, his stark distinction and negative valuation of Hagar sets up a harmful duality that might be exploited by anybody, including contemporary preachers for nefarious purposes. A postcolonial homiletical exegesis can help to make some sense of these contradictions and ambiguities by making the complex colonial context more visible.

Biblical scholar Stephen Moore has also studied Paul's epistles from a postcolonial perspective. He has pointed out how Paul's message often seems full of "ambivalence, incoherence, and self-subversion—and not least where its message of emancipation subtly mutates into oppression."[36] When it comes to preaching from Paul's epistles, part of the problem is the partial critique of colonial realities that they contain. For example, in 1 Corinthians, Paul condemns going to prostitutes (6:15–16) but does not criticize the sexual uses of slaves.[37] This rather ambiguous view of slavery becomes especially uncomfortable for contemporary postcolonial readers when he uses it as a theological metaphor to describe Christians' relationship with Christ, asserting that Christians "were bought with a price" (1 Cor. 6:20; 7:23). Such a metaphor not only implicitly accepts the system of slavery in terms of endorsing the buying and selling of people but also raises the painful question of sex slavery. Hagar, who was a slave, may have experienced triple slavery, once by Abraham and Sarah, second by Paul, and third by us, unless we read her differently.

In conclusion, the church has too often been complicit with colonialism and its more recent manifestation, neoliberal transnational capitalism. Those of us who are privileged as academic practitioners of postcolonial biblical interpretation need to engage and learn from the experience of social, cultural, and economic others such as Hagar. A postcolonial biblical reading as exegesis for preaching "enables ordinary poor and marginalized people to interpret the biblical text in a manner that foregrounds and emphasizes their own lived experience and contextual realities."[38] Postcolonial preachers have a distinctive role to play in terms of faithfully interrogating and scrutinizing the text as a way of challenging the status quo. Biblical stories like the one about Rahab in Joshua have raised some difficult issues, most critically issues about colonial injustices. Instead of simply glorifying the victors and demonizing the losers, postcolonial preachers can refuse to take the easy way and can invite the congregation to imagine how different groups of people might coexist in the postcolonial context marked by migration and the threat of new forms of slavery.

Moving forward, finally, a postcolonial exegetical process must be communal. The homiletical hermeneutics of the Bible is not a private enterprise. It is to be done by the community, for the community, and with the community. For decades in Latin America and Africa, the community-engaged grassroots' Bible study has played a pivotal role in shaping liberation theology and decolonizing movements.[39] Even if a preacher engages the text alone, he or she does so in a way that is very conscious of his or her community, their needs, and responses to the biblical text. The voice that is missing from the text, voices that are often missing from the contemporary discussion writ large, maybe adequately lifted up and heard in this reading strategy.

SERMON EXAMPLE

The following sermon, as an example that addresses neoliberal capitalism, makes an intriguing connection between the shepherd and his employer as the owner of the sheep. It challenges the status quo interpretation of the parable and encourages a communitarian reading of the Bible while lifting up the voices that were unheard. Since postcolonial preaching is still new in homiletics, it is not easy to find many sermons that explicitly use a contrapuntal reading strategy. Pablo Jiménez, however, is one of the pioneering scholars who paved a path in postcolonial preaching. His sermons offer valuable examples of how a postcolonial exegesis can be done. His sermon entitled "The Pearl," found in *Pulpito*,[40] is particularly noteworthy. This sermon was preached bilingually in both English and Spanish. It is an intercultural sermon that deploys two different messages in two distinct languages. The worship setting of his homily is the installation service of a pastor Iluminado Castello at Emmanuel Christian Church in Mentor, Ohio.

In "The Pearl," Jiménez preaches from Matt. 13:45-46: "Again, the kingdom of heaven is like a merchant in search of fine pearls; on finding one pearl of great value, he went and sold all that he had and bought it." Jiménez first describes the parable as "scandalous." Its aim, he says, is "to shatter our way of understanding the world, inviting us to accept a new way of seeing and understanding reality" (112). To bring this reality into focus, he considers another similar parable, the parable of the lost sheep (Luke 15). Jiménez contests the conventional interpretation of this parable that sees God as the shepherd who rescues us every time we stray. He, scandalously, denies that the parable is about God's unconditional love and the shepherd's guaranteed protection. I argue here that he deploys a contrapuntal reading strategy as he invites the congregation to see the shepherd in a different light. He writes, "We must bear in mind that most shepherds were not the owners of the sheep" (113). As discussed earlier, the goal of a contrapuntal reading is not to be content with the dominant and obvious point of view but to reveal the hidden and less obvious issues that are intermeshed in the story's entangled colonial and master-slave relationships. Instead of assuming that the shepherd is a powerful and protective figure, Jiménez reveals the colonial system that is intermeshed in the story, where the shepherd as the colonized seems to be doing the work for the ruling class. Allowing this possibility to come to the fore, he invites the congregation to become the shepherd in this story: "Now, be honest with me, if you were caring for a hundred sheep and you lost only one, would you risk losing the other ninety-nine?" (113). Of course, we would not risk the ninety-nine and our own safety for the sake of the one. Economically it does not make sense. Neither does it make sense ethically. Furthermore, we would not jeopardize losing our job as a shepherd knowing how angry the colonial owners of the sheep would be. Then Jiménez provides the final punch line: "The message of the parable of the lost sheep is not about unconditional love, but about risk. The loving shepherd is willing to risk the well-being of the ninety-nine sheep and, thus, his own well-being, for the lost sheep. Through the parable, God calls us to risk our all for the kingdom of God" (114). Finally, then, he connects this parable with the parable of the pearl hat also teaches that "we must be willing to abandon everything for the sake of the kingdom" (115) because he has spent all he had to keep the pearl.

This is a great example of the use of a contrapuntal reading strategy for postcolonial preaching. Jiménez's sermon opens the eyes of the congregation to the socioeconomic reality facing many of us in today's world and challenges us to risk changing that order rather than to receive God's protection and care passively and comfortably. The sermon encourages the pastor, Iluminado Castellano, to become a shepherd, taking risks in leading his flock for the sake of the realm of God.

NOTES

1. Fred Craddock, *Preaching* (Nashville: Abingdon, 1985), 52.
2. Segovia, "And They Began to Speak in Other Tongues," 29–30.
3. Gonzalez, "Minority Preaching in a Postmodern Age," 190.
4. Mary Ann Tolbert, "Reading for Liberation," in *Reading from this Place: Social Location and Biblical Interpretation in the United States*, ed. Fernando F. Segovia and Mary Ann Tolbert (Minneapolis: Fortress, 1995), 275.
5. Segovia, "And They Began to Speak in Other Tongues," 8.
6. Austin Phelps, *The Theory of Preaching: Lectures in Homiletics* (New York: Scribner's, 1894), 39. HyeRan Kim-Cragg, "Probing the Pulpit," 22–30.
7. Harry Stout, "Puritan Preaching," in *Concise Encyclopedia of Preaching*, ed. William Willimon and Richard Lischer (Louisville: Westminster/John Knox, 1995), 394–395.

8. Gregory, "Expository," 382.
9. Rose, *Sharing the Word*, 13.
10. Gregory, "Expository," 383.
11. Tolbert, "Reading for Liberation," 275.
12. Gonzalez, "Minority Preaching in a Postmodern Age," 188.
13. Stephen Slemon, "Modernism's Last Post," in *A Postmodern Reader*, ed. J. Natoly and L. Hutcheon (Albany: SUNY, 1993), 431.
14. Tolbert, "Reading for Liberation," 269.
15. Allen, *Preaching the Other: Studies of Postmodern Insights* (St. Louis: Chalice, 2014), 21.
16. Said, *Culture and Imperialism*, 51.
17. Jacques Derrida, *Of Grammatology*, translated by Gayatri Chakravorty Spivak (Baltimore & London: Johns Hopkins University Press, 1976).
18. David Buttrick, *Homiletic: Moves and Structures* (Philadelphia: Fortress, 1980), 47.
19. Said, *Culture and Imperialism*, 51.
20. Ibid., 66.
21. Other biblical scholars organize these principles in a similar vein: behind, of, in front of the text. Sandra M. Schneiders, *The Revelatory Text: Interpreting the New Testament as Sacred Scripture*, 2nd edition (Collegeville: Liturgical Press, 1999); Robert Kysar and Joseph M. Webb, *Preaching to Postmoderns: New Perspectives for Proclaiming the Message* (Peabody, Mass: Hendrickson Publishers, 2006).
22. Segovia, "And They Began to Speak in Other Tongues," 13.
23. Musa Dube, *Postcolonial Feminist Interpretation of the Bible* (St. Louis: Chalice, 2000), 60.
24. Paulo Freire, *The Pedagogy of the Oppressed* (New York: Seabury, 1973), 104.
25. Elsa Tamez, "The Bible and the Five Hundred Years of Conquest," in *Voices from the Margins*, 8–9.
26. Mary Louise Pratt, *Imperial Eyes: Travel Writing and Transculturation* (New York: Routledge, 1992), 6–7.
27. Dube, *Postcolonial Feminist Interpretation of the Bible*, 60.
28. Laura Donaldson, "Postcolonialism and Bible Reading," *Semeia* 75 (1996): 11.
29. Dube, *Postcolonial Feminist Interpretation of the Bible*, 201.
30. Allen, *I will Tell You the Mystery*, xxvii.
31. Mary Rose D'Angelo, "Theology in Mark and Q: Abba and 'Father' in Context," *Harvard Theological Review* 85 (1992): 174.
32. Mary Rose D'Angelo, "Abba and 'Father': Imperial Theology and the Jesus Traditions," *Journal of Biblical Literature* 111 (1992): 623.
33. Kwok, *Discovering the Bible in a Non-Biblical World*, 88.
34. Kwok, *Postcolonial Imagination and Feminist Theology*, 90.
35. Donaldson, "Postcolonialism and Bible Reading," 8.
36. Stephen Moore, *Empire and Apocalypse: Postcolonialism and the New Testament* (Sheffield: Sheffield, 2006), 31.

37. Sheila Briggs, "Slavery and Gender," in *On the Cutting Edge: The Study of Women in the Biblical Worlds*, ed. Jane Schaberg, Alice Bach, and Esther Fuchs (New York: Continuum, 2003), 171–192.

38. Anthony Reddie, "Foreword," in *Mark and Its Subalterns: A Hermeneutical Paradigm for a Postcolonial Context*, ed. David Joy (London: Equinox, 2008), xi. (xi–xiii).

39. Carlos Mesters, "The Use of the Bible in Christian Communities of the Common People," in *The Challenge of Basic Christian Communities*, ed. Sergio Torres and John Eagleson (Maryknoll: Orbis, 1981), 197–210.

40. Gonzalez and Jiménez, *Pulpito*. Hereafter parenthesis.

Conclusion
What Next?

As a conclusion, not as an end but as an arch toward the future, let me summarize the RIPPLE approach to preaching and identify some areas for further study. The six organizing principles of the RIPPLE approach (Rehearsal, Imagination, Place, Pattern, Language, and Exegesis) can be used to guide crafting of a postcolonial sermon. At the outset, I suggested that the structure of the book itself can be understood as a series of ripples emanating from a stone thrown into the water: sermon as a movement of creating a ripple effect. The central image I had from the beginning was the Gospel as a single stone dropping in water and the ripples going out from it. It does not matter which is first. These principles just travel out each following and relating to the other and getting energy from the other for the sake of preaching the Gospel. The chapters do not build on one another in sequential fashion but work together like ripples on a lake, creating intersecting patterns and concentric circles.

Postcolonial preaching as "Rehearsal" assumes and supports the claim that preaching needs to be always reforming. A postcolonial preacher ought to pose such self-examining questions as: How does our preaching support and embody justice and peace in the world? What preaching patterns and styles do we use that will lead to the fulfillment of God's realm on earth?

The very gesture of self-scrutiny is a daily discipline of imagining a new world through the rehearsal of the realm of God in the preaching act. The preaching "Imagination" is to proclaim that another world is not only possible but also is already here because it is rehearsed. This other world, God's realm based on justice, equity, and peace, is the world where the last shall be first and the hungry shall be invited to the heavenly banquet. For the preaching imagination to be a rehearsal, we must constantly practice what we believe and know. By our fruit, people will recognize who we are (Matt. 7:16). How Christians behave toward one another matters. Not only do these behaviors proclaim the gospel among Christians but they make the gospel known to the world.

This lived reality of the preaching world is key to the postcolonial preaching concept of "Place." A critical review of the United States and Canada as settler colonial states as the foundational space of the preaching place has demonstrated that racism and colonial history must be taken seriously in order to effectively preach the Gospel. The discussion of the preaching place also led to realize how much global migration could potentially effect the practice of preaching and the place of preaching. This is where new awareness of the intercultural place of preaching comes in. In this regard, new preaching places can be deconstructed and reconstructed to address the needs of a postcolonial congregation with its complex cultural, linguistic, and racial identities of congregants and preachers.

A critical examination of the preaching "Place" is enhanced when one critically examines colonial preaching from the pulpit where the expository Puritan Plain style became the most dominant preaching "Pattern" during the British colonialism of the nineteenth and twentieth centuries in North America. Examining various patterns, it has become apparent to the readers how old and existing patterns are still relevant even if they also have limitations. For instance, using the deductive sermon pattern, the preacher's relationship to the congregation is often hierarchical. However, it is well suited if the sermon is to invite repentance of the congregation from colonial abusive power, and challenge or renew the congregation's worldview, its identity, and its mission. In the inductive sermon pattern, the preacher is in a relationship of collegiality with the congregation. At its best, the inductive pattern leads congregations to a place where a different worldview is anticipated, while at its worst, it is confusing and wrongly takes for granted a higher level of biblical and theological literacy that may not exist. The bottom line is that knowing the strengths and the limitations of various patterns and adopting them in nimble ways is essential and key to postcolonial preaching.

In dealing with the "Language" of preaching, I have tried to overcome Anglo-centered preaching by introducing non-Western and non-colonial languages including, but not limited to, Korean and Chinese. Postcolonial preaching promotes a proclamatory practice that gives voice to expansive and inclusive use of multiple languages. The languages we employ in preaching matter to persons with disabilities and to those who are marginalized due to race, class, gender, sexual orientation, and colonial violence. A polyglot approach to preaching is foundational to the postcolonial sermon. To be a polyglot as a postcolonial preacher does not mean actually being able to speak several languages; however, laudable that may be (and some preachers in many parts of the world such as Europe and colonized contexts are multilingual). Rather, to be a postcolonial polyglot preacher means that one is intentionally reaching across linguistic and cultural boundaries to identify with others who are different from you. Here language is understood as the extension of being. Don Wardlaw eloquently captures this point: "To speak in another's tongue is to be given the capacity to identify closely with the other person and to find the sensitivity to be open to the other person's need. Speaking in the tongues of other seekers at Pentecost, then, means among other things entering deeply into their lives to promote *shalom,* or wholeness."[1]

Furthermore, we cannot fully understand the impact of cultural imperialism through English as the colonial language without examining dominant biblical interpretation as a tool to impart Eurocentric Christian hegemony. Here the role of "Exegesis" becomes critical. Preaching strategies reflect particular experiences arising from postcolonial places and migration contexts. In examining texts about Rahab in Joshua and in Paul's letters to the Galatians and Corinthians, as well as Jesus's naming God as *Abba* in the context of the Roman Empire, a contrapuntal postcolonial reading of scripture has proved to be a useful tool for negotiating gender, authority, citizenship, ethnicity, race, and class as these issues arise in the Bible.

Given the fact that a postcolonial approach to homiletics is still at a forming stage, what is presented in this book is modest and is meant simply to get preachers thinking about how to live out their vocation in the current neocolonial context. It is my hope that those who are in the process of preparing sermons for their congregations may use the RIPPLE approach as a kind of checklist with which to approach this rather big and complex task, venturing into an unchartered homiletical territory. The questions below can be raised in sermon preparation alone, or with congregations, and also as a way of getting feedback following a sermon. The checklist can also be used as a way to think through homiletical exegesis. Having a checklist handy also serves as a steady and constant practice like brushing teeth or taking vitamins in the morning as a necessary exercise in healthy living.

REHEARSAL

- How does the selected text anticipate a new world, the realm of God?
- Where is a sign of that new world being rehearsed in the life of the congregation or in local and international events?
- What are some concrete practices as sermon examples that can be shared as the good news and as a spiritual and regular action?

IMAGINATION

- Can you picture the text? Can you hear the text? Are there smells that are evoked by the story? Can you describe your main message in sensory ways?
- Can you find poetic, musical, and other literary examples that encourage people to grasp the reality based on justice, mercy, and equity as alternative?
- Make sure to include concrete examples from experiences that are conducive to stir up imagination. These are often captured in Psalms and contemporary poetry.

PLACE

- What did you notice about the place in the biblical text in light of colonial reality?
- Can you make a connection between the place in the text and a place where the congregation is located?
- How do both biblical and congregational places reflect and represent the plight and the promise of the migration realty?

PATTERN

- What pattern among existing patterns may work for the sermon you and your congregation are working on crafting?
- Do you see a pattern emerging from the biblical text in terms of the way it is told?
- Have you considered how a certain pattern you are inclined to may be exclusive to those who are in the pew?

LANGUAGE

- Is there a word, a doctrine, and or a concept drawing your attention from postcolonial optics?
- Have you tried to incorporate languages other than your own in the sermon, languages that may be the mother tongue of others in your congregation, for example?
- Have you addressed the issue of colonial, racist, discriminatory, and biased language?

EXEGESIS

- What commentary (if any) have you used and is this commentary faithfully and justly examining colonial reality?
- What effort have you made finding the missing and marginalized voices in the story?
- Have you tried to engage congregations (lay members, newcomers) and those outside the congregation you serve?

The given checklist of questions is not exhaustive. But it may give us a place to start. As Chinese philosopher Lu Xun eloquently put it, "hope is like a path in the countryside: originally there was no path—yet, as people are walking all the time across the same spot, a way appears." It is my hope that others join this journey. The path is barely trodden as yet. And there is a long way to go, not to mention potential branches to explore.

One such branch to be explored is the impact of racism in homiletics. In this regard, there are some scholars in the Academy of Homiletics who set out to work on an anthology entitled *Unmasking Whiteness in Preaching* following the annual conference under the same theme in 2019. This is a welcome development. Another urgent branch on the path of postcolonial preaching is the ecological crisis. There is growing interest on the part of scholars in ecological theology, eco-feminist ethics, and biblical studies in animal hermeneutics. An example of this is the Earth Bible series and the Season of Creation Commentary series. Homiletics as an inter-disciplinary and cross-disciplinary field is in a good position to engage and promote robust conversation with these growing areas of study. Practitioners of homiletics and people in the pew will welcome such a conversation. Some of them may already be implementing and experimenting with such an endeavor. We are also encouraged that the Festival of Homiletics 2020 has chosen the theme of ecology and preaching. Attention to racism and ecological violence is closely related and highly beneficial to postcolonial preaching because moving beyond colonialism requires attention to these issues.

Finally, this book is coming to press in the midst of the COVID-19 outbreak. This global pandemic has changed the very act of preaching around the world. The so-called Zoom worship has become the norm in many places. Online worship is going to be more common than ever. The way we have always done preaching is gone. Preachers in the COVID era or the post-COVID era must learn to proclaim the Gospel virtually. Preachers and worship leaders must wrestle with the lack of physical intimacy in the preaching act when congregations cannot verbally sing and do the call and response. Preachers need to grapple with the challenge of how preaching can still accomplish an aspect of pastoral care when preachers cannot easily or immediately feel the needs of the congregation while preaching.

A gift of postcolonial preaching proposed here is that it aims to be flexible, resisting rigidity and contesting the status quo. As the East Asian ideogram meaning "crisis," combined with two words, 危機 (wee-kee), aptly captures, such events bring danger or threat "危" but can also provide an opportunity "機" with possibilities. It is my hope that preachers are ready to tackle the COVID-19 crisis with urgency and danger, anchored in hope and resilience with possibilities.

NOTE

1. Don Wardlaw, "Preaching as the Interface of Two Social Worlds," 83.

Afterword

While the purpose of this book was to instill concepts of postcolonial thought within those who take preaching seriously in the twenty-first century, this book makes a much broader contribution to the field of homiletics. With the final edits being done in the middle of the COVID-19 pandemic, the continuing pandemic of racism, and a time when anti-immigration sentiments are high, "Postcolonial Preaching" takes on a new level of importance. The coronavirus has forced worship and preaching to undergo major and abrupt changes as we move to online formats. But those changes also open our churches to the possibility of a global congregation. The face of Christianity is changing with Korean missionaries in Mexico and Kazakhstan, a growing number of Pacific Islanders in seminaries, and the rapid growth of Christianity in Africa. Already climate change is forcing people in hotter climates to migrate north to seek food security and survival. This will only increase in the future. The spirituality they bring with them is rich and varied and essential for the wholeness of who we are as the body of Christ. "Postcolonial Preaching" is not a text for the periphery of a preacher's library but should be at the core of seminary homiletical education as we prepare preachers for an unknown future. Moving into the unknown requires forward-looking, all-inclusive, compassionate resources that start with those on the margins of whatever communities in which we are engaged. The suffering in our world is immense. What good news will we have to offer for those whose suffering is deeply rooted in oppressive systems of colonialism, slavery, and Eurocentrism?

Rev. Dr. Kathy Black
Claremont School of Theology
August 2020

Bibliography

Ahmed, Sara. *Strange Encounters: Embodied Others in Post-Coloniality*. New York: Routledge, 2000.
Allen, Ronald J. "The Social Function of Language." In *Preaching as a Social Act: Theology and Practice*, edited by Arthur Van Seters, 167–203. Abingdon: Nashville, 1988.
———. *Patterns of Preaching: A Sermon Sampler*. St. Louis: Chalice, 1998.
———. *Interpreting the Gospel: An Introduction to Preaching*. St. Louis: Chalice, 1998.
———. "Preaching as Mutual Critical Correlation through Conversation." In *Purposes of Preaching*, edited by Jana Childers, 1–22. St. Louis: Chalice, 2004.
———. *Preaching and the Other: Studies of Postmodern Insights*. St. Louis: Chalice, 2009.
———. *I Will Tell You the Mystery: A Commentary on Preaching the Book of Revelation*. Eugene: Cascade, 2019.
Allen, O. Wesley Jr. "The Pillars of the New Homiletic." In *The Renewed Homiletic*, edited by O. Wesley Allen Jr., 1–18. Minneapolis: Fortress, 2010.
Ashcroft, Bill, et al. *The Empire Writes Back: Theory and Practice in Post-Colonial Literature*. New York: Routledge, 1989.
Bailey, Randall, Benny Liew, and F. Segovia, eds. *They Were All Together in One Place? Toward Minority Biblical Criticism*. Atlanta: Society of Biblical Literature, 2009.
Barnes, Jonathan, ed. *The Complete Works of Aristotle*. Princeton: Princeton University Press, 1984.
Bartow, Charles. *The Preaching Moment*. Nashville: Abingdon, 1980.
Bernal, Martin. *Black Athena: Afroasiatic Roots of Classical Civilization Vol I: The Fabrication of Ancient Greece 1785–1985*. London: Free Association Books, 1987.
Bhabha, Homi. *The Location of Culture*. New York: Routledge, 1994.

Bieler, Andrea, HyeRan Kim-Cragg, Isolde Karle, and Ilona Nord, eds. *Religion and Migration: Negotiating Hospitality, Agency and Vulnerability*. Leipzig: EVA, 2019.
Black, Kathy. *A Healing Homiletic: Preaching ad Disability*. Nashville: Abingdon, 1996.
Bland, Dave L. "Deductive." In *New Interpreter's Handbook of Preaching*, edited by Paul Scott Wilson, 375–377. Nashville: Abingdon, 2008.
Bonhoeffer, Dietrich. *Worldly Preaching*. New York: Thomas Nelson, 1975.
Briggs, Sheila. "Slavery and Gender." In *On the Cutting Edge: The Study of Women in the Biblical Worlds*, edited by Jane Schaberg, et al., 171–192. New York: Continuum, 2003.
Bronfenbrenner, Urie. *The Ecology of Human Development: Experiment by Nature and Design*. Cambridge: Harvard University Press, 1979.
Brown, Teresa Fry. *Delivering the Sermon: Voice, Body, and Animation in Proclamation*. Minneapolis: Fortress, 2008.
Brueggemann, Walter. *Finally Comes the Poet*. Minneapolis: Fortress, 1989.
———. *Text Under Negotiation: The Bible and Postmodern Imagination*. Minneapolis: Fortress, 1993.
———. *The Practice of Prophetic Imagination: Preaching an Emancipatory Word*. Minneapolis: Fortress, 2012.
Burke, Kenneth. *A Grammar of Motives*. Berkeley: University of California Press, 1959.
Burkhart, John E. *Worship: A Searching Examination of the Liturgical Experience*. Philadelphia: Westminster Press, 1982.
Buttrick, David. *Homiletic: Moves and Structures*. Philadelphia: Fortress, 1987.
Campbell, Charles L. "Inductive Preaching." In *Concise Encyclopedia of Preaching*, edited by William H. Willimon, et al., 270–272. Louisville: Westminster John Knox, 1995.
Campbell, Charles L. and Johan H. Cilliers. *Preaching Fools: The Gospel as a Rhetoric of Folly*. Waco: Baylor University Press, 2012.
Carvalhaes, Claudio. "Storytelling Renewed." In *The Renewed Homiletic*, edited by O. Wesley Allen Jr., 35–39. Minneapolis: Fortress, 2010.
Celebrate God's Presence: A Book of Services for The United Church of Canada. Toronto: United Church Publishing House, 2000.
Childers, Jana and Clayton Schmit, eds. *Performance in Preaching: Bringing the Sermon to Life*. Grand Rapids: Baker, 2008.
Choi, Woosung Calvin. *Preaching to Multiethnic Congregation: Positive Marginality as a Homiletical Paradigm*. New York: Peter Lang, 2015.
Condon, John C., et al. *An Introduction to Intercultural Communication*. New York: Macmillan, 1987.
Congar, Yves. "Sacramental Worship and Preaching." In *The Renewal of Preaching: Theory and Practice, Vol. 33 of Concilium*, edited by Karl Rahner, translated by Theodore L. Westow, 51–63. New York: Paulist, 1968.
Cooper, Burton Z. and John McClure. *Claiming Theology in the Pulpit*. Louisville: Westminster John Knox, 2003.

Couture, Pamela, et al., eds. *Complex Identities in a Shifting World: Practical Theological Perspectives*. Zurich: LIT, 2015.
Craddock, Fred. *As One Without Authority*. Nashville: Abingdon, 1971.
———. *Preaching*. Nashville: Abingdon, 1985.
Craigo-Snell, Shannon. *The Empty Church: Theology, Theatre and Embodied of Hope*. Oxford: Oxford University Press, 2014.
Crawford, Evans E., et al. *The Hum: Call and Response in African American Preaching*. Nashville: Abingdon, 1995.
Davis, H. Grady. *Design for Preaching*. Minneapolis: Fortress, 1958.
Davis, Kenneth G. "Cross-Cultural Preaching." In *Preaching and Culture in Latino Congregations*, edited by Kenneth G. Davis and Jorge L. Presmanes, 41–61. Liturgical Training Publication, 2000.
Davis, Kenneth G. and Jorge L. Presmanes, eds. *Preaching and Culture in Latino Congregations*. Chicago: Liturgy Training, 2000.
Davis, Ossie. "The English Language Is My Enemy." In *Revelations: An Anthology of Expository Essays by and about Blacks*, edited by Teresa M. Reed, 163–164. Needham Heights: Ginn Press, 1991.
D'Angelo, Mary Rose. "Theology in Mark and Q: Abba and 'Father' in Context." *Harvard Theological Review* 85 (1992): 149–174.
———. "Abba and 'Father': Imperial Theology and the Jesus Traditions." *Journal of Biblical Literature* 111:4 (1992): 611–630.
Derrida, Jacques. *Of Grammatology*. Translated by Gayatri Chakravorty Spivak. Baltimore: Johns Hopkins University Press, 1976.
Dieter, Otto. "Arbor Picta: The Medieval Tree of Preaching." *Quarterly Journal of Speech* 51 (1965): 123–144.
Donaldson, Laura. "Postcolonialism and Bible Reading." *Semeia* 75 (1996): 1–14.
Dorniseh, Loretta. "Symbolic Systems and the Interpretation of Scripture: An Introduction to the Work of Paul Ricoeur." *Semeia* 4 (1975): 1–26.
Dube, Musa. *Postcolonial Feminist Interpretation of the Bible*. St. Louis: Chalice, 2000.
Duck, Ruth. *Worship for the Whole People of God: Vital Worship for the 21st Century*. Louisville: Westminster John Knox, 2013.
Dykstra, Craig and Bass, Dorothy. "A Theological Understanding of Christian Practices." In *Practicing Theology: Beliefs and Practices in Christian Life*, edited by Miroslav Volf and Dorothy Bass, 13–32. Grand Rapids: Eerdmans, 2002.
Edwards Jr., O. C. "Puritan Plain Style." In *New Interpreter's Handbook of Preaching*, edited by Paul Scott Wilson, 410–411. Nashville: Abingdon, 2008.
Elizondo, Virgilio. *Galilean Journey*. Maryknoll: Orbis, 1983.
———. *The Future is Mestizo: Life where Cultures Meet*. Revised edition. Boulder, Colo.: University Press of Colorado, 2000.
Eslinger, Richard. *A New Hearing: Living Options in Homiletic Method*. Minneapolis: Fortress, 1987.
Fernandez, Eleazar. "The Geopolitical and the Glocal: Situating Global Theological Voices in Theological Education." In *Teaching Global Theologies: Power and*

Praxis, edited by Kwok Pui-lan, Cecelia Gonzalez-Andrieu, and Dwight N. Hopkins, 163–176. Waco: Baylor University, 2015.

Fiorenza, Elizabeth Schüssler. *In Memory of Her: A Feminist Theological Reconstruction of Christian Origins*. New York: Crossroad, 1994.

Fischer, Kathleen. *The Inner Rainbow: The Imagination in Christian Life*. New York: Paulist Press, 1983.

Florence, Anna Carter. *Preaching as Testimony*. Louisville: Westminster John Knox, 2007.

———. "Preaching Imagination." In *Teaching Preaching as Christian Practice*, edited by Thomas Long and Leonora Tubbs Tisdale, 116–133. Louisville: Westminster/John Knox, 2008.

———. *Rehearsing Scripture: Discovering God's Word in Community*. Grand Rapids: Eerdmans, 2018.

Foster, Cecil. *They Call Me George: The Untold Story of Black Train Porters and the Birth of Modern Canada*. Winsor: Biblioasis, 2019.

Freire, Paulo. *The Pedagogy of the Oppressed*. New York: Seabury, 1973.

Go, Yohan, et al. "Making New Spaces in Between: A Post-Reflective Essay Weaving Postcolonial Threads into North American Homiletics." *Homiletic* 40:1 (2015): 56–62.

Goldenberg, David M. Goldenberg. *The Curse of Ham: Race and Slavery in Early Judaism, Christianity, and Islam*. New Jersey: Princeton University Press, 2005.

González, Justo. "Minority Preaching in a Postmodern Age." In *Sharing Heaven's Music: The Heart of Christian Preaching: Essays in Honor of James Earl Massey*, edited by Barry L. Callen, 183–190. Nashville: Abingdon Press, 1995.

———. "By the River of Babylon." In *Preaching Justice: Ethnic and Cultural Perspectives*, edited by Christine Smith, 80–97. Cleveland: United Church Press, 1998.

———. and Jiménez, Pablo. *Pulpito: An Introduction to Hispanic Preaching*. Nashville: Abingdon, 2005.

Gordon, Milton. *Assimilation in American Life: The Role of Race, Religion, and National Origin*. New York: Oxford University Press, 1964.

Gregory, Joel C. "Expository." In *New Interpreter's Handbook of Preaching*, edited by Paul Scott Wilson, 381–383. Nashville: Abingdon, 2008.

Green, Garret. *Imaging God: Theology and the Religious Imagination*. San Francisco: Harper & Row 1989.

Hall, Stuart. "When Was the 'Post-Colonial?' Thinking at the Limit." In *The Post-Colonial Question: Common Skies, Divided Horizons*, edited by Iain Chambers and Lidia Curri, 242–260. London: Routledge, 1996.

Haraway, Donna. "The Promises of Monsters: A Regenerative Politics for Inappropriate/d Others." In *Cultural Studies*, edited by Lawrence Grossberg, Gary Nelson, and Paul Treichler, 295–337. New York: Routledge, 1992.

Harris, Maria. *Fashion Me a People: Curriculum in the Church*. Louisville: Westminster John Knox, 1989.

Hauser, W. Kurt. *Invisible Slaves: The Victims and Perpetrators of Modern-Day Slavery*. Stanford: Stanford University Hoover Institution Press, 2017.

Haynes, Stephen R. *Noah's Curse: The Biblical Justification of American Slavery.* Oxford: Oxford University Press, 2002.
Held, Shirley E. *Weaving: A Handbook for Fiber Craftsmen.* New York: Holt, Rinehart & Winston, 1973.
Hilkert, Mary. *Naming Grace: Preaching and the Sacramental Imagination.* New York: Continuum, 1997.
Holbert, John C. *Preaching Creation: The Environment and the Pulpit.* Eugene: Cascade, 2011.
Isasi-Diaz, Ada Maria. "Solidarity: Love of the Neighbor in 1980s." In *Life Every Voice: Constructing Christian Theologies from the Underside,* edited by Susan Brooks Thistlethwaite and Mary Potter Engel, 31–40. San Francisco: Harper and Row, 1990.
Jiménez, Pablo. "In Search of a Hispanic Model of Biblical Interpretation." *Journal of Hispanic/Latino Theology* 3:2 (November 1995): 44–64.
Joh, Wonhee Anne. *Heart of the Cross: A Postcolonial Christology.* Louisville: Westminster John Knox, 2006.
Keck, Leander E. *The Bible in the Pulpit.* Nashville: Abingdon, 1978.
Keller, Catherine. *From a Broken Web: Separation, Sexism and Self.* Boston: Beacon Press, 1986.
———. *Face of the Deep: A Theology of Becoming.* New York: Routledge, 2003.
Keller, Catherine, et al. *Postcolonial Theologies: Divinity and Empire.* St. Louis: Chalice, 2004.
Kim, Eunjoo Mary. *Preaching the Presence of God: A Homiletic from an Asian American Perspective.* Valley Forge: Judson, 1999.
———. *Preaching in an Age of Globalization.* Louisville: Westminster John Knox, 2010.
Kim, Matthew D. "A Blindspot in Homiletics: Preaching That Exegetes Ethnicity." In *Journal of the Evangelical Homiletics Society* 11:1 (March 2011): 66–83.
———. "The World of Ethnic and Cultural Issues in Preaching." In *The Worlds of the Preacher: Navigating Biblical Cultural and Personal Contexts,* edited by Scott M. Gibson, 73–88. Grand Rapids: Baker, 2018.
Kim-Cragg, HyeRan. S*tory and Song: A Postcolonial Interplay between Christian Education and Worship.* New York: Peter Lang, 2012.
Kim-Cragg, HyeRan and Joanne Doi. "Intercultural Threads of Hybridity and Threshold Spaces of Learning." *Religious Education* 107:3 (2012): 262–275.
Kim-Cragg, HyeRan and Eunyoung Choi. *The Encounters: Retelling the Bible from Migration and Intercultural Perspectives.* Daejeon: Daejanggan, 2013.
———. "Between and Beyond Asian-ness: A Voice of a Postcolonial Hybrid Korean-Canadian in the Diaspora." In *What Young Asian Theologians Are Thinking: the CSCA Christianity in Southeast Asia Series No 7,* edited by Leow Theng Huat, 90–102. Singapore, Trinity Theological College, 2014.
Kim-Cragg, HyeRan and Mai-Anh Le Tran. "Turning to the Other: Interdenominational, Interethnic, Interreligious Activism and A New Ecclesia." In *Complex Identities in a Shifting World: One God and Many Stories,* edited by Pamela Couture, Robert

Mager, Pamela McCarroll, and Natalie Wigg-Stevenson, 127–138. Zurich: LIT, 2015.

———. "Postcolonial Practices on Eucharist." In *Postcolonial Practice of Ministry: Leadership, Liturgy, and Interfaith Engagement*, edited by Kwok Pu-lan and Stephen Burns, 77–89. Lanham: Lexington, 2016.

———. *Interdependence: A Postcolonial Feminist Practical Theology*. Eugene: Pickwick, 2018.

———. "Unfinished and Unfolding Tasks of Preaching: Interdisciplinary, Intercultural, and Interreligious Approaches in the Postcolonial Context of Migration." *Homiletic* 44:2 (2019): 4–17.

———. "Probing the Pulpit: Postcolonial Feminist Perspectives." *Liturgy* 34:2 (2019): 22–30.

———. "Power and Practice of Indigenous Christian Rituals and Ceremonies." In *Honourable Reconciliation*, edited by Paul Gareau and Don Schweitzer. Regina: University of Regina Press, forthcoming.

Kwok, Pui-Lan. *Discovering the Bible in a Non-Biblical World*. Maryknoll: Orbis, 1995.

———. *Postcolonial Imagination and Feminist Theology*. Louisville: Westminster/John Knox, 2005.

———. "Postcolonial Preaching in Intercultural Contexts." *Homiletic* 40:1 (2015): 8–21.

———. "Epilogue." In *Postcolonial Practice of Ministry: Leadership, Liturgy, and Interfaith Engagement*, edited by Kwok Pui-lan and Stephen Burns, 215–222. Lanham: Lexington, 2016.

Kwok, Pui-Lan and Stephen Burns, eds. *Practice of Ministry: Leadership, Liturgy, and Interfaith Engagement*. Lanham: Lexington, 2016.

Kysar, Robert and Joseph M. Webb. *Preaching to Postmoderns: New Perspectives for Proclaiming the Message*. Hendrickson: Peabody, 2006.

Lange, Dirk G. and Dwight W. Vogel, eds. *Ordo: Bath, Word, Prayer, Table—A Liturgical Primer in Honor of Gordon W. Lathrop*. Akron: OSL, 2005.

LaRue, Cleophus J. *The Heart of Black Preaching*. Louisville: Westminster John Knox, 2000.

Lee, Boyung. *Transforming Congregations through Community: Faith Formation from the Seminary to the Church*. Louisville: Westminster John Knox, 2013.

Liew, Tat-siong, Benny. *What is Asian American Biblical Hermeneutics? Reading the New Testament*. Honolulu: University of Hawai'i Press, 2008.

Long, Thomas G. "Preaching God's Future: The Eschatological Context of Christian Proclamation." In *Sharing Heaven's Music: The Heart of Christian Preaching, Essays in Honor of James Earl Massey*, edited by Barry L. Callen, 191–202. Nashville: Abingdon Press, 1995.

———. *The Witness of Preaching*. Louisville: Westminster/John Knox, 2005.

Long, Thomas G. and Nora Tisdale, eds. *Teaching Preaching as a Christian Practice: A New Approach to Homiletical Pedagogy*, edited by Thomas Long and Leonora Tubbs Tisdale, 3–17. Louisville: Westminster John Knox, 2008.

Lord, Jennifer. "Sacraments, Preaching and Teaching Of." In *New Interpreter's Handbook of Preaching*, edited by Paul Scott Wilson, 284–285. Nashville: Abingdon, 2008.

Lowe, Lisa. *Immigration Act: On Asian American Cultural Politics*. Durham: Duke University Press, 1996.

Lowry, Eugene L. "The Revolution of Sermonic Shape." In *Listening to the Word: Studies in Honor of Fred. B. Craddock*, edited by Gail O's Day and Thomas Long, 93–112. Nashville: Abingdon, 1993.

———. *The Homiletical Plot: The Sermon as Narrative Art Form*. Louisville: Westminster John Knox, 2001.

Lugard, John D. Frederick. *The Dual Mandate in British Tropical Africa*. Edinburgh: Blackwood, 1922.

Matsuoka, Fumitaka. *Learning to Speak a New Tongue: Imagining a Way that Holds People Together-An Asian American Conversation*. Eugene: Pickwick, 2011.

McClure, John. *The Roundtable Pulpit: Where Leadership and Preaching Meet*. Nashville: Abingdon, 1995.

———. "Expository Preaching." In *Concise Encyclopedia of Preaching*, edited by William Willimon and Richard Lischer, 130–132. Louisville: Westminster John Knox, 1995.

———. *Other-wise Preaching: A Postmodern ethic for Homiletics*. St. Louis: Chalice Press, 2001.

———. *Preaching Words: 144 Key Terms in Homiletics*. Louisville: Westminster John Knox, 2007.

McFague, Sallie. "An Earthly Theological Agenda." In *Ecofeminism and the Sacred*, edited by Carol Adams, 84–98. New York: Continuum, 1993.

Medina, Néstor, Alison Hari-Singh, and HyeRan Kim-Cragg, eds. *Reading in Between: How Minoritized Cultural Communities Interpret the Bible in Canada*. Eugene: Pickwick, 2019.

Mesters, Carlos. "The Use of the Bible in Christian Communities of the Common People." In *The Challenge of Basic Christian Communities*, edited by Sergio Torres and John Eagleson, 197–210. Maryknoll: Orbis, 1981.

Meyers, Carol. *Rediscovering Eve: Ancient Israelite Women in Context*. Oxford: Oxford University Press, 2013.

Mitchell, Henry. *Black Preaching*. New York: Harper and Row, 1970.

———. *Black Belief: Folk Beliefs of Blacks and America and West Africa*. New York: Harper & Row, 1975.

———. *Celebration and Experience in Preaching*. Nashville: Abingdon, 1991.

———. "The Hearer's Experience of the Word." In *Listening to the Word: Studies in Honor of Fred B. Craddock*, edited by Gail R. O' Day and Thomas G. Long, 223–241. Nashville: Abingdon, 1993.

Moore, Mary Elizabeth Moore. *Teaching as a Sacramental Act*. Cleveland: Pilgrim Press, 2004.

Moore, Stephen. *Empire and Apocalypse: Postcolonialism and the New Testament*. Sheffield: Sheffield, 2006.

Moore, Stephen and Mayra Rivera, eds. *Planetary Loves: Spivak, Postcoloniality, and Theology.* New York: Fordham University Press, 2011.

Morton, Nelle. *Journey Is Home.* Boston: Beacon, 1985.

Mumford, Debra J. "Slavery Prosperity Gospel." *Homiletic* 41:1 (2016): 31–41.

The Murphy Center for Liturgical Research. *Made, Not Born: New Perspectives on Christian Initiation and the Catechumenate.* Notre Dame: University of Notre Dame Press, 1976.

Nieman James R. and Thomas Rogers. *Preaching to Every Pew: Cross-Cultural Strategies.* Minneapolis: Fortress, 2001.

Otto, Beatrice. *Fools are Everywhere: The Court Jester Around the World.* Chicago: University of Chicago, 2001.

Ottoni-Wilhelm, Dawn. "New Hermeneutic, New Homiletic, and New Directions: An U.S.–North American Perspective." *Homiletic* 35:1 (2010): 17–31.

Phelps, Austin. *The Theory of Preaching: Lectures in Homiletics.* New York: Scribner's, 1894.

Power, David N. "The Holy Spirit: Scripture, Tradition, and Interpretation." In *Keeping the Faith: Essays to Mark the Centenary of Lux Mundi,* edited by Geoffrey Wainwright, 152–178. Philadelphia: Fortress, 1988.

Pratt, Mary Louise. *Imperial Eyes: Travel Writing and Transculturation.* New York: Routledge, 1992.

Reddie, Anthony. "Foreword." In David Joy, *Mark and its Subalterns: A Hermeneutical Paradigm for a Postcolonial Context,* xi–xiii. London: Equinox, 2008.

Ricoeur, Paul. *Interpretation Theory: Discourse and the Surplus of Meaning.* Fort Worth: Texas Christian University Press, 1976.

———. *Time and Narrative.* Volume 1, trans. Kathleen McLaughlin and David Pellauer. Chicago: University of Chicago Press, 1984.

Rivera, Mayra. *The Touch of Transcendence: A Postcolonial Theology of God.* Louisville: Westminster John Knox, 2007.

Rose, Lucy Atkinson. *Sharing the Word: Preaching in the Roundtable Church.* Louisville: Westminster John Knox, 1997.

Said, Edward. *Orientalism.* New York: Knopf, 1978.

———. *Culture and Imperialism.* New York: Knopf, 1993.

Saliers, Don E. *Worship as Theology: Foretastes of Glory Divine.* Nashville: Abingdon 1994.

Schade, Leah E. *Creation-Crisis Preaching: Ecology, Theology, and the Pulpit.* St. Louis: Chalice, 2015.

Schneiders, Sandra M. *The Revelatory Text: Interpreting the New Testament as Sacred Scripture.* 2nd edition. Collegeville: Liturgical Press, 1999.

Schumemann, Alexander. *The Eucharist: Sacrament of the Kingdom.* Crestwood, N.Y.: St. Vladimir's Seminary Press, 1988.

Seed, Patricia. *Ceremonies of Possession in Europe's Conquest of the New World, 1492–1640.* Cambridge: Cambridge University Press, 1995.

Segovia, Fernando F. "And They Began to Speak in Other Tongues." In *Reading from This Place: Social Location and Biblical Interpretation in the United States,*

Vol. 1, edited by Fernando F. Segovia and Mary Ann Tolbert, 1–32. Minneapolis: Fortress, 1995.

Slemon, 431 in J. Natoly and L. Hutcheon, eds. *A Postmodern Reader*. Albany: SUNY, 1993.

Smith, Christine. *Weaving the Sermon: Preaching in a Feminist Perspective*. Louisville: Westminster/John Knox, 1989.

———. *Preaching as Weeping, Confession, and Resistance: Radical Responses to Radical Evil*. Louisville: Westminster John Knox, 1992.

———. "Feminist Preaching." In *Concise Encyclopedia of Preaching*, edited by William H. Willimon and Richard Lischer, 134–136. Louisville: Westminster John Knox, 1995.

Smith, Sarah J. *Hearing Sermon: Reader-Response Theory as a Basis for a Listener-Response Homiletic*. PhD dissertation, Emmanuel College, University of Toronto, 2002.

Snyder, Susanna, Brazal, Agnes M., and Ralston, Joshua, eds. *Church in an Age of Migration: A Moving Body*. New York: Palgrave, 2015.

Spivak, Gayatri C. *In Other Worlds: Essays in Cultural Politics*. New York: Methuen, 1987.

———. "Can the Subaltern Speak?." In *Marxism and the Interpretation of Culture*, edited by Cary Nelson and Lawrence Grossberg, 271–313. Urbana: University of Illinois Press, 1988.

———. "The Post-Colonial Critic." In *The Post-Colonial Critic: Interviews, Strategies, Dialogues*, edited by S. Harasym, 67–74, New York: Routledge, 1990.

———. *Outside in the Teaching Machine*. New York: Routledge, 1993.

———. *A Critique of Postcolonial Reason: Toward a History of the Vanishing Present*. Cambridge: Harvard University Press, 1999.

Stout, Harry. "Puritan Preaching." In *Concise Encyclopedia of Preaching*, edited by William Willimon and Richard Lischer, 394–397. Louisville: Westminster/John Knox, 1995.

Sugirtharajah, R. S., ed. *Voices from the Margins: Interpreting the Bible in the Third World*. London: SPCK, 1995.

———. *The Postcolonial Bible*. Sheffield: Sheffield Academic Press, 1998.

———. *The Vernacular Hermeneutics: The Bible and Postcolonialism 2*. Sheffield: Sheffield Academic Press, 1999.

———. *The Bible and The Third World: Postcolonial Encounters*. Cambridge: Cambridge University Press, 2001.

———. *Postcolonial Reconfigurations*. St. Louis: Chalice Press, 2003.

Tamez, Elsa. "The Bible and the Five Hundred Years of Conquest." In *Voices from the Margin: Interpreting the Bible in the Third World*, edited by R. S. Sugirtharajah, 1–18. Maryknoll: Orbis, 2016.

Taylor, Barbara Brown. "Preaching the Body." In *Listening to the Word: Studies in Honor of Fred B. Craddock*, edited by Gail R. O' Day and Thomas G. Long, 210–211. Nashville: Abingdon, 1993.

Taylor, Diane. *The Archives and the Repertoire: Performing Cultural Memory in the Americas*. Durham: Duke University Press, 2003.

Thomas, Frank. "The Truth Is Always Relevant: Race and Economics in Contemporary African American Preaching." *Homiletic* 41:1 (2016): 42–56.

Thompson, Lawrence and Winnick, R. H. *Robert Frost*. New York: Holt, Rinehart & Winston, 1981.

Tisdale, Leonora Tubbs. *Preaching as Local Theology and Folk Art*. Minneapolis: Fortress, 1997.

Tolbert, Mary Ann. "Reading for Liberation." In *Reading from this Place: Social Location and Biblical Interpretation in the United States*, edited by Fernando Segovia and Mary Ann Tolbert, 263–276. Minneapolis: Fortress, 1995.

Travis, Sarah. *Decolonizing Preaching: The Pulpit as Postcolonial Space*. Eugene: Cascade, 2014.

Trible, Phyllis. *God and the Rhetoric of Sexuality*. Philadelphia: Fortress, 1978.

Troeger, Tom. "Can You Imagine This? The Future Role of Imagination in Preaching." In *Breaking on the Brink: The Future of Homiletics*, edited by Martha Simmons, 135–144. Nashville: Abingdon, 1996.

Turner, Mary Donovan. "Reversal of Fortune: The Performance of a Prophet." In *Performance in Preaching: Bringing Sermon to Life*, edited by Jana Childers and Clayton Schmit, 87–98. Grand Rapids: Baker, 2008.

Turner, Mary Donovan and Mary Lin Hudson. *Saved from Silence: Finding Women's Voice in Preaching*. St. Louis: Lucas Park, 2014.

Ward, Richard. *Speaking of the Holy: The Art of Communication in Preaching*. St. Louis: Chalice, 2001.

Wardlaw, Don M. "Preaching as the Interface of Two Social Worlds: The Congregation as Corporate Agent in the Act of Preaching." In *Preaching as a Social Act: Theology and Practice*, edited by Arthur Van Seters, 55–93. Abingdon: Nashville, 1988.

———. ed. *Learning Preaching: Understanding and Participating in the Process*. Lincoln: Lincoln College and Seminary Press and the Academy of Homiletics, 1989.

Willobee, Sondra. *The Write Stuff: Crafting Sermons that Captures and Convince*. Louisville: Westminster John Knox, 2009.

Wilson, Paul Scott. *Imagination of the Heart*. Nashville: Abingdon, 1988.

———. *The Practice of Preaching*. Toronto: United Church Publishing House, 1996.

———. *God Sense: Reading the Bible for Preaching*. Nashville: Abingdon, 2001.

———. "New Homiletic." In *New Interpreter's Handbook of Preaching*, edited by Paul Scott Wilson, 398–401. Nashville: Abingdon, 2008.

World Council of Churches. *Baptism, Eucharist, and Ministry*. Geneva: WCC, 1982. Dirk G. Lange and Dwight W. Vogel, eds. *Ordo: Bath, Word, Prayer, Table—A Liturgical Primer in Honor of Gordon W. Lathrop*. Akron: OSL, 2005.

Volf, Miroslav. "Theology for a Way of Life." In *Practicing Theology: Beliefs and Practices in Christian Life*, edited by Miroslav Volf and Dorothy Bass, 245–263. Grand Rapids: Eerdmans, 2002.

Young, Robert J. C. *Colonial Desire: Hybridity in Theory, Culture and Race*. London: Routledge, 1995.

Zimmerman, Michael E. *Contesting Earth's Future: Radical Ecology and Postmodernity*. Berkeley: University of California Press, 1994.

Index

Abba, 100, 115, 116, 121nn31–32, 125
Advent, 17, 29
African-American, 57, 65n38, 68, 72, 77, 78, 86n48, 88, 95
Ahmed, Sara, 25, 65n34
Allen, O. Wesley Jr., 28n31
Allen, Ronald J., 18, 27n13, 71
All my Relations, 100
androcentric, 55, 108, 113
anthropocentrism, 20, 99
apocalyptic, 71, 72
arrojar, 52
Ashcroft, Bill, 3, 11n3

Babel, 87
Bailey, Randall, 65n34
Barnes, Jonathan, 86n38
Bartow, Charles, 27n18
basileia, 13, 16, 17, 22, 24–26
belonging, 24, 39, 48, 54
Bernal, Martin, 52, 64n17
Bethlehem, 22, 26
Bhabha, Homi, 3, 10n2, 45n9, 53, 64n23
Bieler, Andrea, 46n33
bifocal, 38, 79
bilingual, 56, 78, 94
binary, 2, 47, 79
BIPOC, 51

Black, Kathy, 90, 102n10
Black Lives Matter, 36, 51
Bland, Dave L., 69, 84n7, 84n10
body thinking, 89
Bonhoeffer, Dietrich, 102n4
border-crossing, 34, 47
Briggs, Sheila, 122n37
Brown, Teresa Fry, 88, 102n6, 103n12
Brueggemann, Walter, 7, 12n16, 20, 28n28, 34, 45n15, 45n18, 46n35, 90
Burke, Kenneth, 93, 103n20
Burkhart, John E., 15, 27n10
Buttrick, David, 90, 111, 121n18
bystander, 16

Campbell, Charles L., 54, 65n28, 85n19
canonization, 113
Carvalhaes, Claudio, 21, 28n31
Celebrate God's Presence, 27n6
chavah, 92
Childers, Jana., 45n21, 85n28
Chinese Head Tax, 49
Choi, Woosung Calvin, 65n33
chronos, 18
citizenship, 49, 50, 107, 117, 125
civilization, 64n17, 97–99
civil rights movements, 93
colonization, 1, 2, 31, 52, 57, 83, 96, 97, 116

communication, 14, 48, 67, 75–77, 86n39, 93, 98, 102n8, 109
concentric, 123
Condon, John C., 86n39
Congar, Yves, 21, 28n30
consensus, 75, 76
contradiction, 5, 10, 34, 35, 50, 53, 116, 118
contrapuntal, 5, 10, 105–7, 111, 112, 116, 117, 119, 120, 125
conversion, 99, 115
Cooper, Burton Z., 28n34
Couture, Pamela, 11n7
COVID-19, 100–102, 127
Craddock, Fred, 30, 45n7, 70, 85nn15–16, 90, 102n2, 102n5, 103n20, 106, 120n1
Craigo-Snell, Shannon, 7, 11n15, 27n12
Crawford, Evans E., 86n48
Creation Commentary, 127
Cree, 59, 60, 100
crisis, 54, 65n27, 65n30, 102, 127, 128
cross-cultural, 46n34, 78, 86n51, 86n54, 94
cultural imperialism, 4, 50, 96, 125
culturally treasonable, 109, 113
culture, 2

D'Angelo, Mary Rose, 121nn31–32
Davis, H. Grady, 68, 84n3
Davis, Kenneth G., 65n33, 78, 86n51, 86n54
Davis, Ossie, 91, 103n12
deductive, 9, 68–70, 72, 75–78, 84n7, 84n10, 124
Derrida, Jacques, 111, 121n17
dialogical, 31, 36–39
diasporic, 31, 34, 36, 38–40
dichotomy, 21, 51
didactic, 72
Dieter, Otto, 84n9
dislocation, 78
displacement, 22, 30, 34, 39, 52, 78, 113, 114

Donaldson, Laura, 115, 121n28, 121n35
Dorniseh, Loretta, 27n20
Dube, Musa, 114, 115, 121n23, 121n27, 127n29
Duck, Ruth, 27n14
Dykstra, Craig, 27n3

ecclesia, 16, 32
Edwards Jr., O. C., 85n11
egalitarian, 74
Elizondo, Virgilio, 78, 86n52
emphatic, 115
Enlightenment, 69, 97, 107
epistemology, 4, 17
eschatological, 20, 22, 35, 75
Eslinger, Richard, 103n37
ethnicity, 2, 8, 19, 48, 55, 57, 96, 103n29, 107, 117, 125
ethos, 76
Eucharist, 7, 14, 21, 27n5, 28n29, 53
Eurocentric, 4, 53, 92, 125
exegesis, 5, 10, 19, 22, 58, 79, 105–9, 111, 113, 115–19, 121, 123, 125, 127
exile, 25, 39, 71, 115
expository, 9, 69, 70, 72, 75, 77, 85n13, 103n12, 109, 121n8, 121n10, 124
ezer, 92

familia, 116
feminist, 3, 8, 9, 11n4, 12n18, 12n20, 24, 37, 45n3, 46n27, 46n29, 55, 65n34, 68, 72–75, 78, 80, 85n23, 110, 112, 114, 116, 121n23, 121n27, 121n29, 121n34, 127
Fernandez, Eleazar, 63n1
Fiorenza, Elizabeth Schüssler, 46n27
Fischer, Kathleen, 30, 45n4
Florence, Anna Carter, 14, 15, 27n7, 27n9, 27n13, 31, 35, 37, 45n11, 45n24, 45n28
Foster, Cecil, 64n8
Freire, Paulo, 114, 121n24

gaze, 55
globalization, 34

global warming, 54
Go, Yohan, 12n21
Goldenberg, David M., 91, 103n13
Golgotha, 63
González, Justo, 7, 12n17, 64n1, 78, 86n55, 108, 120n3, 121n12, 122n40
Gordon, Milton, 27n5, 64n3
Green, Garret, 45n5
Gregory, Joel C., 121n8, 121n10

Hagar, 25, 117, 118
Hall, Stuart, 39, 46n32
Ham, 91, 103n13
Haraway, Donna, 54, 65n25
Harris, Maria, 27n4
Hauser, W. Kurt, 64n11
Haynes, Stephen R., 103n14
Held, Shirley E., 85n26
hermeneutical, 18, 19, 79, 102, 122n38
heterogeneous, 57
heuristic, 4
hierarchical, 6, 51, 68, 74, 97, 108, 113, 124
Hildegard of Bingen, 69
Hilkert, Mary, 45n22
Hispanic, 51, 78, 86n53, 95
historical criticism, 106–8, 112, 113
historical imagination, 37, 39
Holbert, John C., 85n20
holistic knowing, 75–77
home, 1, 2, 20, 22, 24–26, 30, 32, 33, 39, 40, 42, 44, 48, 49, 52, 55, 83, 86n40, 99, 101, 115
homiletics, 2–4, 6, 9, 10, 12n21, 13, 14, 26n1, 30, 45n12, 52, 64n22, 68, 69, 73, 74, 77, 85n24, 94, 96, 103n29, 105, 117, 119, 120n6, 125, 127
homogenous, 2, 56, 78
hook, 77
hope, 4, 7, 10, 11n15, 16, 17, 30, 35, 37, 38, 41, 43, 44, 53, 62, 79, 87, 101, 125, 127, 128
hospitality, 24, 46n33
host, 40–41
humor, 54

hybridity, 3, 39, 47, 53, 86n42, 103n31

iconoclastic, 4
ideograms, 32, 94
imagination, 5, 7–9, 11n4, 12n16, 12n18, 20, 29–41, 43, 45nn4–5, 45nn10–13, 45n15, 45n18, 45n22, 45n25, 45n29, 45n35, 65n34, 71, 74, 77, 79, 112, 121n34, 123, 126
incarnational, 88
inclusive, 24, 48–50, 90, 92, 93, 98, 99, 124
indigenous, 20, 36, 48, 51, 53, 54, 58–60, 63, 78, 87, 98–100, 110, 114, 115
indirect communication, 75–77
indirect speech, 76
inductive, 9, 68, 70–72, 75, 76, 79, 85n19, 124
innocence, 114
intercultural, 9, 10, 12n19, 34, 45n20, 84n1, 86n39, 86n42, 119, 124
interdependent, 6, 20, 33, 77
interdisciplinary, 2, 12n19, 14, 18, 57, 112
intuition, 76–78
Isasi-Diaz, Ada Maria, 11n11, 24
Islam, 103n13, 118

Jesa, 80
Jiménez, Pablo, 18, 65n33, 78, 79, 86n53, 106, 119, 120, 122
Joh, Wonhee Anne, 11n6
juxtapose, 96

kahkiyaw, 100, 101
Kairos, 13, 17, 18, 47, 63
Keller, Catherine, 11n6, 54, 65n29, 65n34
Kim, Eunjoo Mary, 30, 45n6, 75
Kim, Matthew D., 65n35, 103n29
Kim-Cragg, HyeRan, 11n12, 12nn19–20, 27n15, 28n24, 45n2, 45n8, 46n33, 64n7, 64n9, 65n34, 84n1, 84n5, 85n35, 86n42, 120n6

Kin-dom, 5–7, 10, 11n11, 16, 21, 22, 24–26, 29, 31, 32, 98
Koinonia, 14
Korean War, 43
Kwok, Pui-Lan, 3, 8, 11n4, 11n8, 11n10, 12n18, 31, 34, 36–39, 45n20, 46n26, 46n29, 46n30, 64n1, 65n34, 121n33, 121n34
Kysar, Rober, 121n21

lament, 47
Lange, Dirk G., 27n5
LaRue, Cleophus J., 65n33, 77, 78, 86n46, 89, 102n7
Latina/o, 9, 50, 57, 65n33, 72, 86n51, 86n53
Latinx, 68, 78–80
lectionary, 23, 71
Lee, Boyung, 103n25
Left Behind, 71
legitimacy, 54, 110
Leiturgia, 14
liberal democracy, 50
Liew, Tat-siong, Benny, 38, 46n31, 65n34
liminal, 47
linear temporality, 17
linguistic competency, 10, 87
listening event, 71
literalist, 71
liturgical theology, 14, 15
liturgy, 11n8, 11n10, 12n20, 14, 15, 21, 22, 58, 65n33
logos, 76
Long, Thomas G., 45n11, 85n16, 103n20
Lord, Jennifer, 28n32
lost sheep, 88, 119, 120
Lowe, Lisa, 49, 50, 64n5, 64n10
Lowry, Eugene L., 71, 85n16, 85n18
Lugard, John D. Frederick, 97, 103n30

Magi, 41–44
Magnificat, 32, 35

manly clergy, 109
Mansfield Park, 112
Mass, 12n17, 21, 121n21
Matsuoka, Fumitaka, 45n14
McClure, John, 15, 27n8, 28n34, 58, 64n22, 65n37, 85n24, 85nn12–13
McFague, Sallie, 84n8
Medina, Néstor, 65n34
meditation, 75, 76, 81
medium, 5, 81, 89, 109
Mesters, Carlos, 122n39
mestizo, 78, 86n52
metaphor, 5, 14, 15, 29, 33, 37, 53, 67–69, 73, 90, 118
Meyers, Carol, 103n15
migration, 1, 5, 6, 9, 10, 12n19, 22, 25, 38, 39, 44, 46n33, 48–52, 54–57, 78, 84n1, 98, 118, 124–26
mimetic, 110
mimicry, 3, 8, 48, 53, 54
Minjung, 114
minority, 12n17, 57, 65n34, 101, 110, 120n3, 121n12
Mitchell, Henry, 77, 86n49, 88, 102n5
monologue, 32
Moore, Mary Elizabeth Moore, 35, 45n17, 45n23
Moore, Stephen, 28n33, 118, 121n36
Morton, Nelle, 86n40
multilingual, 94, 125
Mumford, Debra J., 48, 64n2, 64n4
Murphy Center for Liturgical Research, 27n16
muscle memory, 16, 22
mystery, 75, 85n21, 88, 89, 121n30

narrative, 9, 15, 27n21, 35, 37, 39, 48, 70, 72, 75, 79, 85n17, 107, 112, 113, 115
neoliberal, 118, 119
New Homiletic, 65n31, 72, 85n22
Nieman, James R., 46n34, 94, 103n23, 103n26
normalizing, 109

objectivity, 92, 107, 108
Occident, 51
oppositional, 110
oral, 38, 77, 94, 106
Ordo, 14, 27n5
organic unity, 73
organism, 68
Orient, 3, 51
Orientalism, 3, 8, 10n1, 48, 51–53, 64n12, 64n16
Otto, Beatrice, 65n26
Ottoni-Wilhelm, Dawn, 55, 65n31

parables, 20, 95
Paraclet, 99
paradox, 17, 26, 31, 34–36, 53, 111
Pater, 116
pathos, 76
patriarchy, 74, 95, 96, 110, 116
pattern, 4, 5, 9, 16, 20, 27n22, 31, 36, 50, 59, 67–81, 83, 84n2, 85, 87, 112, 114, 123, 124, 126
peace, 5, 16, 20, 24, 26, 34, 43, 44, 94, 95, 100, 123
Pentecost, 125
performance, 7, 15, 45n21, 53, 54, 85n28
pew, 16, 46n34, 55, 71, 103n23, 103n26, 126, 127
Phelps, Austin, 108, 120n6
planetary loves, 22, 28n33
polyglot, 5, 10, 87, 124, 125
polyvocal, 38
postcolonial, 1–10, 11nn3–6, 11nn8–10, 11n12, 12nn18–21, 13, 15, 17–20, 22, 28n24, 29–31, 33, 34, 36–40, 45nn19–20, 46nn25–26, 46n29, 46n31, 47, 48, 50, 52–55, 57, 58, 64n13, 64n19, 65n34, 67–70, 72, 74, 78–80, 85n35, 87–89, 93, 94, 96–98, 105–20, 121n23, 121n27, 121n29, 121n34, 122n38, 123–29, 141
postcolonial interpretation, 34
postcolonial pattern, 72, 79, 80

Power, David N., 20
power differential, 95, 96, 106, 112
power-laden, 110
practice, 3, 4, 6–8, 11n8, 11n10, 11n14, 13–17, 19–21, 24, 27nn2–3, 28n26, 28n30, 29–32, 45n11, 45n16, 45n18, 46n35, 47, 53, 54, 57, 62, 73, 80, 81, 84n6, 86n43, 89–91, 93, 95, 100, 110, 115, 123–25
Pratt, Mary Louise, 114, 121n26
principalities, 29, 52
privilege, 5, 9, 17, 18, 38, 48, 49, 55, 61, 79, 89, 90, 105, 114, 117, 118
prophetic, 2, 20, 45n15, 45n18, 46n35
proportion, 73
proselytization, 99
Protestant, 21, 50, 93
proverb, 79, 95, 96, 100
provisional, 37, 72
public speaking, 89
pulpit, 2, 8, 11n9, 12n20, 20, 27n8, 28n34, 54–56, 58, 65n27, 65n33, 65n37, 70, 85n20, 90, 92, 106, 108, 109, 119, 120n6, 122n40, 124
puritan plain, 69, 85n11, 124
purity, 54, 91

rabbinic law, 61
race, 1, 2, 8, 48, 50, 52, 55, 57, 64n3, 65n38, 83, 91, 96, 97, 103n13, 103n31, 107, 115, 117, 124, 125
racism, 30, 49, 50, 52, 56, 58, 92, 96, 101, 124, 127
Rahab, 107, 113, 115, 118, 125
Ramus, 69
reader-response, 19, 27n23, 113
realm, 7, 11n11, 13, 15–21, 29–33, 57, 63, 74, 83, 92, 95, 120, 123, 125
reconciliation, 53, 69, 87
Reddie, Anthony, 122n38
redemption, 93
Reformed, 22, 93
refugees, 40, 44

rehearsal, 5, 7, 9, 13–23, 25, 27, 29–31, 62, 123, 125
relationality, 73
religion, 1, 6, 46n33
Religious Education Association, 52, 64n3, 72, 83, 100, 110, 117
remembrance, 36
repentance, 59, 61–63, 78, 124
representation, 8, 52
resilience, 73, 79, 128
resistance, 32, 38, 51, 53, 73, 79, 94, 103n17, 103n27, 116
resurrected, 55
Revelation, 25, 63, 71–73, 85n21, 103n11, 106, 115
reversal of fortune, 45n21
rhetoric, 1, 5, 19, 65n28, 69, 76, 86n38, 93, 103n15, 110, 112, 114
rhythm, 37, 73–75, 80
Ricoeur, Paul, 18, 27nn20–21
Riel Uprising, 60
ripple effect, 5, 6, 9, 10, 13, 29, 105, 123
Rivera, Mayra, 11n6, 28n33
Rose, Lucy Atkinson, 58, 65n37, 109, 121n9
Ruach, 10

sacramental, 16, 21, 22, 28n30, 45n17, 45nn22–23
Said, Edward, 3, 10, 10n1, 12n23, 51, 64n12, 107, 111
Saliers, Don E., 15, 27n11
salvific, 75
Samaritan, 67, 81, 83, 84
Schade, Leah E., 55, 65n27, 65n30
Schneiders, Sandra M., 121n21
Schumemann, Alexander, 28n29
second naiveté, 18
Seed, Patricia, 103n36
Segovia, Fernando, 52, 64n18, 65n34, 1f 120, 120n2, 120nn4–5, 121n22
self-disclosure, 80
self-scrutiny, 123
settler, 19, 47, 55, 59, 60, 87, 97, 124

sexist, 73, 91, 92, 95, 116
sexuality, 103n15, 110, 117
Shakespeare, William, 62
shalom, 62, 95, 125
shock of recognition, 89
sign language, 9, 90
skenow, 106
slavery, 48–50, 64n2, 64n4, 64n11, 91, 96, 103nn13–14, 107, 109, 113, 117, 118, 122n37
Slemon, Stephen, 110, 121n13
Smith, Christine, 30, 45n3, 73, 74, 85n23, 85n25, 85n27, 85n29, 85n32, 86n55, 92, 96, 103n17, 103n27
Smith, Sarah J., 27n23
Snyder, Susanna, 46n33
social dislocation, 78
social location, 8, 19, 47, 48, 55, 57, 58, 64n18, 79, 113, 117, 120
soteriological, 67
sound, 29, 76, 77, 98, 110, 112, 114, 116
spatial plurality, 17, 67
spectator, 16, 32
spiral, 75, 80
Spivak, Gayatri C., 28n33, 36, 46n25, 52, 64nn19–21, 121n17
status quo, 3, 8, 29, 47, 56, 79, 95, 105, 108, 116, 118, 119, 128
Stout, Harry, 120n7
subaltern, 53, 54, 64n20, 107, 111, 122n38
Sugirtharajah, R. S., 3, 11n5, 34, 45n19, 65n34, 88, 102n1
supersessionist, 92
suspense, 71, 77
Sycamore tree, 59, 63

tabernacle, 106
Table, 21, 22, 27n5
Tamez, Elsa, 121n25
Taylor, Barbara Brown, 88, 102n2
Taylor, Diane, 53, 65n24
terra nullius, 114
testimony, 27n13, 45n24, 46n28

theological body language, 88, 90
theological literacy, 72, 124
Thomas, Frank, 65n38
Thompson, Lawrence, 45n1, 65n20, 65n25
three-point sermon, 69
Tisdale, Leonora Tubbs., 27n2, 45n11, 58, 65n36
Tolbert, Mary Ann, 108, 109
tongue, 45n14, 64n18, 120n2, 120n5, 121n22, 125, 126
tradition, 20, 21, 23, 28n27, 32, 34, 38, 39, 47, 49, 52, 73, 75–77, 82, 87, 91–93, 95, 106, 108, 113, 121n32
traitor, 110
trajectory, 4, 37, 39, 40, 55
transatlantic, 48, 91
transcendence, 11n6
transnationality, 47
trauma, 39
Travis, Sarah, 11n9
treaty, 59, 60
Trible, Phyllis, 103n15
trickster, 8, 48, 54, 55, 59
Troeger, Tom, 34, 45n12, 86n48
truth, 5, 31, 35, 50, 52, 61, 65, 67, 70, 76, 77, 82, 100, 108–10, 112
Turner, Mary Donovan, 35, 45n21, 74, 85n31, 86n40

utterance, 34, 37, 38, 76, 116

vernacular, 88
violence, 1, 5, 36, 38, 44, 50–52, 72–74, 79, 83, 107, 109, 110, 124, 127
vocalization, 78

vocation, 9, 75, 82, 93, 125
voice, 29, 37–40, 42, 50, 52, 53, 57, 59, 89, 93, 95, 109, 110, 112, 114, 116, 119, 124, 127
Volf, Miroslav, 27n3, 28n26
vulnerability, 54, 89

Ward, Richard, 89, 102n8
Wardlaw, Don M., 6, 11n14, 26n1, 125, 128n1
warp, 74
weaving, 73, 74
weft, 74
whiteness, 64n14
white supremacy, 1, 8, 52, 108
wholeness, 7, 73, 125
Willobee, Sondra, 77, 86n45
Wilson, Paul Scott, 12n22, 28n32, 45n10, 45n13, 51, 72, 84nn6–7, 85n11, 85n22, 86n43
witness, 10, 14, 16, 27n17, 34, 61, 79, 84, 101, 106, 107, 110
witty agency, 54
womanist, 113, 114
word, 6, 14, 21, 22, 27n5, 27n7, 35, 45n15, 65n37, 68, 85n16, 88–90, 93, 102n2, 102n5, 103n20, 106, 121n9
World Council of Churches, 27n5
worldliness, 113

Yin and Yang eyes, 79
Young, Robert J. C., 97, 103n31

Zacchaeus, 59–63
Zimmerman, Michael E., 65n25

About the Author

HyeRan Kim-Cragg holds the inaugural Timothy Eaton Memorial Church Professorship in Preaching, Emmanuel College of Victoria University at the University of Toronto, Canada. She is conscious of her hybrid identities captured in the hyphen, Korean-Canadian, Kim-Cragg, and racialized migrant settler in Canada. Committed to an interdisciplinary approach to homiletics in practical theology, she has written on a wide range of topics related to biblical interpretation, postcolonial theories, feminist homiletics and liturgy, migration, and anti-racism and whiteness. Along with her monographs, *Story and Song* (2012) and *Interdependence* (2018), and her coauthored books, *Hebrews* (2015) and *What Does the Bible Say?* (2017), her publications have appeared in various journals, *Homiletic*, *International Journal of Homiletics*, *Liturgy*, and *Religious Education*, and in edited volumes, including *Liturgy in Postcolonial Perspectives* (2015), *Postcolonial Practice of Ministry* (2016), and *The Rowman & Littlefield Handbook on Women's Studies in Religion* (2021).

www.ingramcontent.com/pod-product-compliance
Lightning Source LLC
Chambersburg PA
CBHW050909300426
44111CB00010B/1445